The Centrality of Jesus Christ

Spirituality and Society

The Centrality of Jesus Christ

GRAHAM JOSEPH HILL

Eagna Publishing • Sydney, Australia

THE CENTRALITY OF JESUS CHRIST

Published by: Eagna Publishing (Sydney, Australia)
eagnapublishing@icloud.com
Cover and interior design: Graham Joseph Hill
www.grahamjosephhill.com

paperback isbn: 978-1-7643311-7-3
ebook isbn: 978-1-7643311-8-0
version number: 2025-12-01

NATIONAL LIBRARY OF AUSTRALIA

A catalogue record for this book is available from the National Library of Australia

Contents

Introduction: Jesus Christ as the Center in an Age of Drift

The church hums with life, activity, and complexity. Sanctuaries and living rooms, prayer circles and pulpits, online gatherings and weary hearts: every space carries its delights and its wounds. Beneath the sermons and the songs, beneath the ambitions and anxieties of Christian life, something holy still pulses. There's a heartbeat beneath the noise and nostalgia, a presence that the church's distractions can't extinguish. Christ still walks among us. Yet few of us slow long enough to see.

We live in an age of spiritual velocity. Our calendars overflow, our convictions fray, our communities fracture. The world moves faster than our capacity for attention. Our hands scroll while our hearts sleep. We mistake certitude for faithfulness, tribal belonging for discipleship, charisma for holiness, and visibility for fruitfulness. In this restless age, the centrality of Jesus can feel like a familiar slogan we've learned to repeat but forgotten to embody. And yet, even here, Christ waits.

This book is written for those who sense the drift, for those who feel the ache of faith distorted by politics, personality, fear, and performance. It's for those who long to be gathered again around the One whose self-giving love reveals the truth of God and the truth of our humanity. *The Centrality of Jesus Christ* belongs to the *Spirituality and Society* series, which explores how the way of Jesus shapes the inner life and calls us into courageous engagement with the world. These reflections first appeared on my Substack, *Spirituality and Society with Hilly*, and they're gathered here as a single conversation: an attempt to hear what the Spirit is saying to the churches amid the clamour of our age.

1

The Desert Within the Church

We're not the first generation to wrestle with spiritual barrenness. The prophets knew what it meant to live among ruins and still proclaim hope. Ezekiel looked upon a valley of bones and asked, *Can these bones live?* Isaiah confronted a people drunk on idols (security, power, prestige) and called them back to living water. Jesus walked among religious leaders and spiritual seekers, revealing that the kingdom of God was already among them: hidden, unassuming, yet relentless.

We're witnessing another great unraveling. Churches shrink; trust erodes; leaders fall; communities fracture; meaning thins. The gods of our age (nationalism, individualism, celebrity, grievance, and algorithmic outrage) promise clarity but deliver captivity. We worship influence and neglect integrity. We build platforms and forget people experiencing poverty who sweep the edges of our programs. We curate perfect theological identities while shame metastasizes.

But what if this unraveling isn't death? What if it's descent? The mystics taught that divine love sometimes withdraws its comforts not to punish but to purify, to burn away false centers so that a more genuine, humbler faith can emerge. Perhaps this is our dark night, stripping away the idols that once propped up our confidence. Maybe grace is hidden in this dismantling, calling us back to the One whose cross silences every false promise of power and prestige.

Christ in the Fractures

If the desert mothers and fathers fled to solitude to rediscover God, our wilderness is the church itself, caught between fear and hope, anger and longing. But Christ has never abandoned fractured communities. He walks into locked rooms. He meets doubters, deniers, exiles, and prodigals. He tends the wounded and confronts the proud. He heals, overturns, restores, and re-centers.

To follow him now is to cultivate attention in a culture that monetizes outrage. It's to kneel in humility when the world rewards

2

dominance. It's to carry a cruciform love through spaces haunted by fear. A Christ-centered people don't flee the wounds of the world or the church; they enter them with tenderness and truth. Christ doesn't call us to be conquerors but companions, not empire-builders but witnesses.

But devotion alone is insufficient if it doesn't reshape life. Contemplation must give birth to courage. Silence must give rise to confession. Worship must summon us into justice. The prophets and the mystics must meet again: Moses, who met God in fire, and confronted Pharaoh; Mary, who pondered mystery, and proclaimed revolution.

The Idols That Displace Christ

Every age fashions its own idols. Ours are polished and plausible. They appear as theological correctness, political identity, charismatic personalities, nostalgia, innovation, certainty, purity, and progress. They say that they'll steady us. They promise security, belonging, clarity, and control.

But fear, not faith, feeds them.

And fear is lethal to love.

At the cross, Christ exposes the futility of our false centers. At the resurrection, Christ unveils a new creation where the weak are honored, the proud are humbled, the wounded are welcomed, and the dead are raised.

If we're to follow Christ in this age, we must name these idols honestly, in our systems, our leaders, our churches, and ourselves. We must learn again what it means to be human: creatures of dust and glory, beloved yet limited, stewards rather than masters.

Hope in the Ruins

Yes, there are ruins. Ecclesial ruins. Moral ruins. Emotional ruins. But Scripture insists that resurrection begins precisely in ruins. The risen Christ appeared not in palaces but in gardens and locked rooms, among the grieving, the frightened, the doubting. His body still bore wounds.

This is our hope, not sentiment but resurrection faith: the stubborn conviction that Christ is present in the fractures, working life from what seems irredeemable. I see resurrection in survivors naming truth with courage. I see it in churches confronting narcissism instead of rewarding it. I see it in believers who refuse to scapegoat others, who practice costly solidarity across deep divides, who keep their allegiance anchored in Christ rather than tribe or ideology.

The Invitation

This book isn't a manual or manifesto. It's a pilgrimage, a gathering of reflections born from prayer, lament, and longing. It invites you to re-center your imagination on Jesus Christ: crucified, risen, and reigning.

The journey moves through three movements: the crisis and longing of our age; the depth and discernment of Christ-shaped discipleship; and the cruciform love that rises to heal a wounded world.

The invitation is simple, though never easy:

Return to the Center.

Return to Christ.

Let every idol be exposed, every false allegiance fall away, every fear be met with love.

The question isn't whether Christ is present.

The question is: *Will we turn toward him again?*

PART I — CHRIST AND THE CRISIS OF OUR AGE: DIAGNOSIS AND LONGING

Part I explores the wounds and longings of our age (anger, fractured identity, disillusionment, and doubt) and reveals how these crises expose our hunger to return to Christ as the true center of our lives and communities.

1. The Death of Vengeance, the Birth of Grace: Unlearning the Language of Vengeance

The language of vengeance has become fluent in our time. It fills our feeds, our politics, our conversations. It thrives in the chants of rallies, the venom of comment threads, and the conversations of resentment at family tables. Its grammar is simple: They hurt us, so we must hurt them back. It promises strength, vindication, and balance. It seduces wounded hearts with the illusion of power. But what it delivers is far more sinister: the slow corrosion of our humanity, the distortion of our spirituality, and the unraveling of our common life.

The language of vengeance (whether used by the left, right, progressives, conservatives, or whoever) is dangerous because it's extraordinarily permissive and offers a moral injunction for "holy or righteous" violence (which always ends up as dehumanizing, unholy, and unrighteous violence).[1] We must offer another language that reflects the life, sacrifice, and reconciliation of Jesus Christ.

---

[1] Ezra Klein makes this point about the language of vengeance and its permissiveness, as well as the moral injunction for violence, in the September 19, 2025, episode of the Ezra Klein Show, "Spencer Cox Wants to Pull Our Politics Back From the Brink."

Vengeance corrupts because it shrinks the other into a caricature. No longer neighbor, no longer image-bearer, but enemy. In this exchange, we lose more than we gain. When we fixate on settling scores, we mirror the very violence that wounded us. Bitterness hardens like ice around the soul until compassion freezes and joy disappears. Vengeance doesn't heal the wound; it deepens it. It leaves scar tissue where tenderness might have grown.

It's no surprise that vengeance also poisons the spirit. To harbor revenge is to kneel at a false altar, enthroning our pain as judge and executioner. We place ourselves in God's seat, wielding judgment with clenched fists. But Scripture resounds with another word: "Vengeance is mine, says the Lord."[2] Ultimate justice belongs not to our rage but to divine mercy. When we grasp for vengeance, we choke grace and cut ourselves off from the peace of prayer. The restless heart can't listen to God while rehearsing hatred.

Nor is vengeance confined to individuals. It metastasizes into society itself. Nations speak it when leaders weaponize fear, when mobs are rallied to punish, when policies are built on retribution rather than restoration. A culture that glorifies vengeance always needs an enemy, and once it finds one, it can't stop. Democracy withers. Justice bends. Neighbors become combatants. History is littered with the ruins of societies undone by vengeance's tongue.

Into this world so fluent in revenge, Jesus Christ speaks another language. He names vengeance for what it is (a lie) and then offers the way of mercy. "You've heard it said, 'Love your neighbor and hate your enemy.' But I say to you, love your enemies and pray for those who persecute you."[3] At the cross, he doesn't curse his executioners but intercedes for their forgiveness. In that moment of unspeakable agony, he unmasks vengeance as powerless and reveals love as the only force that breaks the cycle of retribution.[4]

---

[2] Deut 32:35; Rom 12:19.
[3] Matt 5:43–44.
[4] Luke 23:34.

7

The way of Jesus isn't naïve. It doesn't deny evil. It confronts it with a weapon the world can't comprehend: self-giving love. It resists oppression without mirroring it. It names violence without succumbing to it. It holds to truth without abandoning mercy. To speak the language of Christ is to declare that enemies are still neighbors, that wounds can be healed, that justice and compassion belong together.

Our world is thirsty for vengeance, but vengeance never quenches. Only living water does. The invitation of Jesus is clear: lay down the sword, loosen the tongue of hatred, and learn again the strange, disruptive, healing speech of grace. This is the word that restores our humanity, renews our spirituality, and rebuilds our fractured society.

To understand why vengeance-talk is so dangerous, we must see how it corrupts us from the inside out and how it spreads like wildfire through society.

"Vengeance always promises to heal the wound, but it never does. It only deepens the cut, leaving scar tissue where compassion might have grown."

Poisoning the Heart: How Vengeance Corrupts Our Humanity

When we let vengeance guide our thoughts and words, something in us begins to twist. Our humanity (our capacity for empathy, compassion, and reason) starts to erode. Revenge language frames other people as one-dimensional villains rather than fellow human beings. In doing so, we also dehumanize ourselves. We begin to harden our hearts to empathy and mercy.

Resentment is like a cold anger that settles into the soul and hardens around the heart like ice. Living in a posture of vengeance, we gradually lose the ability to feel joy or kindness. Everything becomes an extension of the fight.

"The thirst for revenge doesn't make us strong; it makes us smaller. The more we fixate on our enemies, the more we become their mirror image."

Have you noticed how a person consumed by bitterness loses their spark? Their world shrinks to the score they must settle. Vengeance promises satisfaction but delivers a shriveling of the spirit. Instead of finding freedom, we become chained to past hurts. Our very identity can wrap around our wound until we define ourselves by opposition to an "enemy." We often become the mirror image of what we hate.

But, answering hate with hate is no true resistance at all: we end up conquered by the very darkness we hoped to destroy. This is the tragic irony: the more we speak and live in vengeance, the more we come to resemble that which wronged us.

A Crisis of the Spirit: How Vengeance Corrupts Our Spirituality

The damage goes even deeper, to the level of the spirit. Harboring vengeance is utterly at odds with the life of the spirit; it pulls us away from Divine love. The core of Christian spirituality centers on transforming the heart toward love, mercy, and humility. But the language of vengeance is a spiritual toxin that breeds hatred and pride. When we thirst for revenge, we effectively shut the door to grace.

We're taught "Vengeance is mine; I'll repay," says God. In other words, ultimate justice belongs to God, not us. Taking vengeance into our own hands (even if only in our speech and fantasies) puts us in God's seat of judgment. This is a form of spiritual idolatry: making an idol of our own sense of justice. It warps our spiritual life into a hollow shell: we might still perform religious duties, but our hearts remain captive to anger.

Moreover, vengeance blocks us from genuine prayer. It's hard to sincerely pray for our daily bread or for forgiveness while clinging to rage against others. And it's impossible to experience the peace of the Holy Spirit while nursing thoughts of harm. Our souls become restless, agitated by the continuous replay of offense and retaliation.

"To speak vengeance is to pray to a false god. Every word of hatred we harbor builds an altar to our own pride, and every sacrifice on that altar drives us further from the living God."

Spiritual leaders have long taught that love and hate can't dwell in the same heart.[5] We have to choose which language our soul will speak. If we select vengeance, we drive out compassion and muffle the voice of God within us. We risk losing the very tenderness and openness that attune us to Christ's voice. In short, vengeance corrupts our spirituality by cutting us off from the source of love and life.

The Social Cancer: How Vengeance Corrupts Society

The language of vengeance doesn't stay confined to individual hearts; it spreads like a contagion through families, communities, political movements, and entire nations. When revenge becomes culturally acceptable, even applauded, the social fabric begins to unravel. We see it in our public discourse: opponents are demonized, and threats replace dialogue.

> *"A culture that speaks vengeance will always need an enemy. It can't rest until it finds one, and once it does, it can't stop until everyone becomes one."*

Vengeful rhetoric in the political arena encourages people to view their neighbors as enemies. We hear it when leaders at podiums vow "judgment day" for their rivals or brag, "this will be our revenge." Crowds cheer, energized by the thrill of vanquishing a foe, but meanwhile, the common good is eroded. Even societies that fancy themselves peaceful aren't immune when fear and anger are stoked.

This vengeful ethos can infect anyone (left or right, progressive or conservative, powerless or powerful): any group that decides another group is a threat or less than human. Once vengeance becomes the driving narrative, mercy and moderation are cast aside. Social divisions harden, and conflict escalates in a vicious cycle: one side's retaliation becomes the next side's provocation. History shows that blood feuds and tit-for-tat violence can persist for generations, destroying countless lives and opportunities for flourishing.

---

[5] Merton, *New Seeds of Contemplation*.

In broader society, the language of vengeance fuels policies of harsh retribution. Justice systems often prioritize punishment over restoration. Leaders justify war and violence as righteous crusades. Fear and rage are constantly inflamed because a community obsessed with vengeance always needs an enemy to blame.

Ultimately, communities lose their sense of shared humanity. People forget how to weep together or to see one another's suffering as their own. Vengeance turns neighbors into combatants and makes peace nearly impossible. It's truly a social cancer, eating away trust, empathy, and the possibility of healing.

The Way of Jesus: A Contradiction to Vengeance

Into this world so fluent in vengeance, Jesus of Nazareth spoke a radically different language. Everything about the way, message, and example of Jesus contradicts the language of vengeance. Where vengeance says, "Hate those who hurt you," Jesus says, "Love your enemies." Where vengeance demands, "Repay evil with evil," Jesus teaches, "Overcome evil with good."[6] He not only taught these principles in the Sermon on the Mount, but he lived them out in the most extreme way.

When Jesus was arrested, tortured, and nailed to a cross, he didn't curse his executioners or call down doom upon them. Astonishingly, he prayed for their forgiveness, even excusing them: "They don't know what they're doing."[7] In that moment of ultimate agony, he broke the cycle of vengeance with a word of mercy. This wasn't weakness; it was a spiritual triumph of a completely different sort.

---

[6] Matt 5:43–48; Rom 12:17–21.
[7] Luke 23:34.

Christian faith proclaims that on the cross, the power of vengeance was unmasked and defeated by the greater power of self-giving love. Jesus demonstrated that true strength is shown not in retaliation but in forgiveness and sacrificial love. His resurrection vindicated this way of mercy, declaring that ultimately life and love have the last word over death and hate.

> *"On the cross, Jesus unmasked vengeance as a fraud. He bore its full weight, answered it with mercy, and revealed that only love, not retribution, has the power to end the cycle."*

In following Jesus, the early Christian community embraced this new language. Amid a Roman culture built on honor and revenge, the first followers of Christ formed a counter-culture of forgiveness.[8] They remembered how Jesus said, "Put away your sword," and "Turn the other cheek." They took seriously his command to forgive "seventy times seven."[9] This way of living was utterly perplexing to the surrounding society. Instead of fueling feuds, these people sought reconciliation. They even prayed for their persecutors and returned kindness for the cruelty they had endured. Such practices weren't naive; they were revolutionary. A forgiving community throws a wrench into the expected gears of retaliation. It proclaims to the world that there's another way to respond to evil.

The way of Jesus (this path of enemy-love and mercy) doesn't deny the reality of evil or injustice. Instead, it confronts evil with a different weapon: not violence or revenge, but redemptive suffering and love. In doing so, it preserves our humanity and even has the power to transform the enemy.

---

[8] Kreider, *The Patient Ferment of the Early Church.*
[9] Matt 26:52; 5:38–39; 18:21–22.

Time and again throughout history, oppressors have been changed because their would-be victims chose to respond with unexpected grace instead of vengeance. The path Jesus offers breaks the cycle of retribution by absorbing wrong and responding with creative love. His entire life modeled this prophetic, compassionate resistance to the culture of payback. And he invites us, here and now, to learn this new language in place of vengeance.

Living the Alternative: Practicing a Language of Grace

Knowing that another way is possible, how do we actually resist the language of vengeance in daily life? It takes intentional practice to unlearn the patterns that are so deeply ingrained in our culture and in our own hearts. Here are some practical ways we can oppose vengeance and offer a better alternative through our actions and words:

Cultivate Inner Mercy

Everything starts in the heart. Through prayer, contemplation, and honest self-examination, confront your own anger and pain. Instead of stoking resentment, bring your wounds to God and ask for grace to prefer healing over retaliation. Regular practices like silent meditation, journaling, or even praying for those who have hurt you can slowly disarm the power of vengeance within.

Watch Your Words

Commit to non-vengeful speech. Vengeance often first appears in how we talk about others: through sarcasm, harsh labels, or spiteful jokes. Practice speaking about opponents (or anyone who frustrates you) in a way that honors their humanity. Refuse to join conversations, whether in person or online, that are driven by hatred and revenge. We can still stand firmly for justice without resorting to dehumanizing language. By choosing words of truth and gentleness, we model a different tone in the public square.

Practice Forgiveness Daily

Forgiveness isn't a one-time act but a discipline. In both minor annoyances and deep hurts, train yourself to let go of the "debt" you feel others owe you. This doesn't mean ignoring wrongs or abandoning justice; it means releasing your personal vendetta. Remember that forgiveness ultimately means giving up your claim to revenge. In doing so, you set both yourself and the other person free, and you create space for God's transforming work in both of you.

Pursue Restorative Justice

In the wider society, support approaches to justice that aim for restoration and reconciliation, not merely punishment. Whenever possible, advocate for responses to wrongdoing that seek healing over retribution. For example, some communities bring victims and offenders together for dialogue and mutual understanding, focusing on making things right rather than simply exacting punishment.[10] When we push for mercy within systems of justice, we help shift the culture away from vengeance and toward wholeness.

Learn from Witnesses of Grace

Fill your imagination with stories of people who chose compassion over revenge. Recall how an Amish community, after a terrible schoolhouse shooting, immediately forgave the shooter and even reached out to care for the shooter's family in their grief.[11] Remember how the families of victims in a Charleston church stood up at a hearing and offered words of forgiveness to the assailant who had murdered their loved ones.[12] These acts of grace weren't easy or weak: they were costly and courageous, and they stunned the world. Let such examples remind you that another spirit is possible. Draw courage and inspiration from those who have walked this path before us.

---

[10] Zehr, *The Little Book of Restorative Justice*.
[11] Kraybill et al., *Amish Grace*.
[12] Hawes, *Grace Will Lead Us Home*.

Build Communities of Peace

We need each other to sustain this counter-cultural way of life. Seek to foster a community (perhaps in a faith congregation, a prayer group, or simply among friends) where the language of grace is consistently practiced. Encourage one another to respond to conflicts with creativity and love, rather than with revenge. When tensions arise, be the one to say, "Let's not rush to blame or retaliation; how can we bring healing?" Over time, such communities become a light in a vengeance-weary world: living proof that the cycle of hatred can be broken.

Finally, resisting the language of vengeance is a prophetic act in our world. It's a refusal to conform to the endless cycle of retaliation and instead the courage to chart a new path. This path isn't easy; it requires courage, faith, and often runs against our natural impulses. Yet it's the path where our humanity is restored, our spirituality flourishes, and our society can find healing. In a world shouting for revenge, we're called to be a different voice (kind but clear, firm but gentle, prophetic but gracious) speaking words of truth and mercy. We become, in effect, translators of heaven's language here on earth, showing that love ultimately triumphs over hate.

"To resist vengeance isn't to ignore injustice. It's to fight it with weapons the world can't understand: mercy, forgiveness, humility, patience, and a fierce love that refuses to surrender our humanity."

The allure of vengeance is strong, tapping into our fears and wounds. But the call of Jesus is stronger still, inviting us to lay down the sword and pick up the cross. Every time we choose compassion over revenge, we participate in a little miracle. We break a chain that might have continued for generations. In doing so, we proclaim that evil doesn't get the final word. This is the hope we cling to: that even in dark times, the light of mercy can shine through us.

May we, in our own spheres of influence, choose to speak life instead of death. May we renounce the language of vengeance that only corrupts and destroys. And may we boldly live out the language of grace, which has the power to heal our world.

2. Let's Stop Talking about Masculinity and Start Talking about Discipleship

The masculinity movement is now an entire industry with books, seminars, and speakers. The movement has grown up around notions of "biblical manhood," but in reality, it reinforces worldly ideas of masculinity and femininity. A whole generation of boys and men today are looking for guidance on how to live as men, and the Christian masculinity industry feeds on their feelings of longing and insecurity. Sadly, the solutions it offers cause further damage. Additionally, a lot of the energy behind complementarianism and the search for "clear gender roles" comes from a crisis of masculinity. Instead of digging deeper into Scripture for guidance about how women and men can live as disciples who conform to Christ, the masculinity movement offers cheap and superficial answers, which end up ruining men and their relationships.

The Christian masculinity movement isn't helping men or women. It's damaging young men, and their relationships with others, and it's distracting us from what should be our true focus—discipleship and imitating Christ. Good discipleship based in a right understanding of the gospel calls us to challenge gender roles in dating, marriage, church, and society.

Young men are looking for guidance on how to live well and how to relate to each other and to women. But a hyper-focus on "masculinity" or "femininity" as the pinnacle of discipleship doesn't help. We need to guide men and women toward honoring, respecting, and relating to each other as equal partners and coheirs with Christ, and the church can do this well by helping both men and women become disciples who imitate Christ Jesus. For men (and women) this means helping them discover how they can become fully conformed to Christ, pursuing lives characterized by virtue and the fruit of the Spirit (Gal. 5:22–23). Shifting our focus away from masculinity or femininity to focus on conformity to the image of Christ would go a long way toward helping us all break free of harmful gender theology.

When our churches make this shift, some will ask, "Are you saying you don't think that the differences between women and men are biblical?" This is a challenging question. On the one hand, the Bible doesn't deny that there are differences between women and men, but discerning the nature of these differences isn't easy or clear (and gender roles vary from culture to culture and generation to generation). On the other hand, the Bible isn't focused on "masculinity" or "femininity." So, when we make the nature of gender our focus, we quickly fall into the trap of mirroring worldly ideas of manhood and womanhood. When we focus on "biblical manhood" or "biblical womanhood," our eyes are on the wrong thing. Healthy personal identity grows when we focus on discipleship and conformity to Christ. And when we focus on this kind of discipleship, we also foster healthy relationships between the sexes.

So, if we aren't talking to boys and men about "Christian masculinity" or "biblical manhood" anymore, then what guidance are we giving them? How are we helping them form personal identities and flourish as men? Thankfully, we already have some guides available.

Recently, a major men's conference was held in my city. The keynote speaker offered three talks on what a man of faith should look like. The speaker asserted that a man should be (1) fearless, standing in awe of God and allowing who he is to lead us into living fearlessly; (2) tender, reflecting the justice, kindness, and humility of God; and (3) thankful, recognizing all God has done for us in Christ. This sounds like a beautiful description of discipleship. But it also sounds like a perfect description of a woman of faith. When we see that discipleship is about conformity to Christ regardless of gender, then we will see how virtues like these apply to everyone.

We should notice, also, that when the biblical authors give guidance to men and women about how to relate to each other, their advice isn't a focus on "masculinity" or "femininity." Their guidance could be summarized like this:

Practice mutual submission and honor one another. Understand that you are equal partners and co-laborers with your brothers and sisters. Together, you are coheirs with your brother, Jesus Christ. Live together in a way that witnesses to Christ and his gospel and that maintains the credibility of your witness in an age of unbelief, persecution, immorality, enslavement, and patriarchy. Be attentive to the expectations and norms of your culture—you can't give constant offense and maintain credible witness. But never sacrifice conformity to Christ, your gospel witness, or mutual submission. In your relationships with each other, imitate Christ's love, grace, compassion, gentleness, kindness, humility, self-sacrifice, and so on. Live as a new creation, as a new people in Christ Jesus. In every aspect of your relationships together as women and men seek to glorify Christ and be conformed to his image until he returns.

Healthy personal identity and interpersonal wellbeing develop as we help boys and men live as disciples who conform to the image of Jesus Christ. Disciples like this practice gender equality, mutual submission, and self-sacrificial nurture and honor of others. Only this leads to healthy disciples, churches, marriages, and ministries.

God became a vulnerable and humble human in the incarnation. Jesus Christ understands our humanity in a unique way, and he sacrificed himself for us. That's the scandal of the cross. Jesus is the suffering and crucified servant. He invites us into a life of humility and vulnerability and sacrifice. We follow a vulnerable Messiah, and we must imitate his weakness and his humility. Our aim should be to help men and women understand that a cruciform faith embraces suffering, self-emptying, and vulnerability. In doing so, the humble disciple discovers the power of the cross and resurrection and lives in a manner pleasing to God.

The greatest threats to Christianity today aren't immigration, same-sex marriage, or increasing secularism in Western countries. The greatest threats to Christianity today are greed, pride, idolatry, selfishness, and abuse of power, along with a combative posture in the world, which fears and excludes others. The answer to these problems is to move from fear and exclusion to discipleship and conformity to Jesus Christ. This is everything. From this posture flows the integrity, morality, values, compassion, humility, love, and witness the world needs. The Christian masculinity movement can't do that—only discipleship can.

God predestined his people to be conformed to the image of his Son (Rom. 8:29). Our major difficulty isn't gender roles or lack of "biblical manhood." Our great challenge is our lack of conformity to the image of Christ. Discipleship and conformity go hand in glove. They're inseparable. We don't need more masculine or feminine Christians; we need more disciples. Today, perhaps more than ever, our focus should be on discipleship and conformity to the image of Christ.

It's time to challenge unhealthy gender roles and stereotypes. Let's stop talking about "masculinity" and "femininity"—let's talk about discipleship.

3. Exvangelicals and the Exodus: Spiritual Lessons for Deconstructing Faith

There's a migration unfolding across Western Christianity. You can hear it in the discussions on podcasts, the honesty of social media posts, the long pauses in once-familiar prayers. They call it *deconstruction*: a word that sounds like demolition but often hides something gentler, something more sacred. For many, this journey begins not with rebellion but with heartbreak. It starts when the old answers stop fitting, when the inherited certainties of childhood faith crumble beneath the weight of reality, trauma, or hypocrisy.

This exodus from evangelicalism (or from institutional religion more broadly) isn't unlike Israel's flight from Egypt: bewildering, liberating, dangerous, and holy. To leave behind a spiritual home, even one that has wounded you, is never easy. The wilderness between "what was" and "what's next" stretches wide and dry. But what if this wilderness, this long wandering called deconstruction, isn't a failure of faith but an invitation into more profound knowing? What if doubt isn't the enemy of belief, but its refiner?

The mystics have known this path for centuries. Long before deconstruction became a hashtag, they spoke of unknowing as the narrow gate to divine union. They too wrestled with silence, contradiction, and loss. They too found that the God who seemed to vanish in the dark was in fact waiting there, hidden in mystery.

The Exodus of the Heart

Every generation faces its own Red Sea: the impossible crossing between what it once believed and what it now knows. For exvangelicals, this crossing often means confronting the idols of certainty, control, and triumphalism that have shaped much of modern Western Christianity.

It means naming the pain of betrayal when institutions protect power over people, when theology is used as a weapon, when faith is tangled with nationalism or abuse. It means daring to ask, "Is this really who God is?"

That question, though painful, is profoundly biblical. Abraham argued with God. Jacob wrestled. Job protested. Mary asked how it could be possible. Even Jesus cried out, "My God, my God, why have you forsaken me?" Doubt and lament aren't foreign intruders to faith; they're the heartbeats of faith that refuses to lie.

The mystics called this threshold "the dark night of the soul."[13] St. John of the Cross, imprisoned by his own religious order, wrote that God sometimes withdraws every trace of light so that our love can be purified. We cling to doctrines, feelings, and experiences until they vanish. Then, stripped of spiritual comfort, we're forced to love God for God's own sake, not for what God gives us. It's a terrifying freedom. But it's also the beginning of maturity.

Deconstruction, seen through this mystical lens, isn't the end of belief. It's the death of illusion. It's what happens when faith sheds its borrowed garments and learns to stand naked before mystery.

"We may fear that deconstruction is the death of faith. But it very often isn't. Deconstruction is often the death of illusion. It's the soul's way of shedding what can't hold divine love and mystery."

---

[13] St. John of the Cross, *Dark Night of the Soul.*

The Cloud of Unknowing

In the 14th century, an anonymous English mystic wrote *The Cloud of Unknowing*, a guide for those who longed to know God but found themselves engulfed in doubt. His advice was shocking in its simplicity: "Give up trying to understand God with your mind. Love can reach where thought can't."[14]

He described the soul as standing beneath a vast, dark cloud: a space where reason falters and old images of God dissolve. But this darkness isn't the absence of God; it's the excess of God. The light is too bright for our eyes. The truth is too vast for our concepts.

"God's silence isn't absence. It's the excess of presence: too vast for our small words to hold."

For those deconstructing faith, this is good news. You aren't lost; you're being reoriented. The old certainties aren't being destroyed but transfigured. God has not abandoned you; God is dismantling the idols that can't hold divine love.

Simone Weil, the 20th-century philosopher-mystic, once said that the absence of God is the most present thing we can feel.[15] She called this absence "a form of divine attention." God, she believed, withdraws so that we might learn to love what is real, not what is imagined.

In that space of silence, everything becomes prayer: grief, rage, confusion, even disbelief. The cloud of unknowing invites us to stop demanding clarity and to start learning how to wait.

The Idols That Must Fall

Every true faith journey involves demolition. The prophets knew this. Before they could rebuild the temple, they had to tear down the high places. Before resurrection, there must be crucifixion.

For many exvangelicals, the idols that must fall aren't golden calves but systems of control disguised as certainty:

---

14 Anonymous, *The Cloud of Unknowing.*
15 Weil, *Waiting for God.*

The idol of power: when faith becomes a tool of domination rather than liberation.

The idol of nationalism: when God is draped in a flag and used to bless violence.

The idol of purity: when love is reduced to moral policing and shame.

The idol of certainty: when mystery is feared more than sin.

These idols masquerade as holiness but deform the soul. The mystics warn that God must shatter every false image before we can see the Real. Deconstruction, then, isn't destruction; it's deliverance.

"To leave behind the gods of control, nationalism, certainty, purity, and power isn't to lose faith. We shouldn't assume that. Instead, it's to find God again in freedom and cruciformity."

To leave these idols behind isn't to leave God; it's to leave what we mistook for God. As the desert fathers and mothers taught, detachment is the path to freedom. "The one who has died to everything," they said, "has already risen."

Between Ruin and Revelation

There is a strange beauty in the ruins of a faith once tightly held. When the scaffolding collapses, when prayer feels hollow, when scripture stings instead of soothes, the temptation is to despair. But the mystics recommend "staying in the ruins."

Moses met God in a bush that burned but wasn't consumed. Elijah heard the divine voice not in the earthquake or fire, but in a thin silence. Christ's resurrection came only after the silence of Saturday. In the same way, the death of old faith can be the soil of a new encounter.[16]

Here, the mystic and the exvangelical stand side by side. Both know the ache of absence and the disorientation of starting over. Both learn that God isn't contained in the language of the past.

Deconstruction isn't unbelief; it's the refusal to live with half-truths. It's the courage to let faith be reborn in truth rather than in fear.

---

[16] Exodus 3:1–6; 1 Kings 19:11–13.

But what comes after?

Reconstruction: The Long Obedience of Love

If deconstruction is the exodus, then reconstruction is the promised land. But this land isn't milk and honey; it's humility, simplicity, and compassion. It's a faith stripped of triumphalism and reborn in tenderness.

Reconstruction doesn't mean returning to certainty. It means learning to live with trust. It's the slow, sacred work of rebuilding a house for the soul on a firmer foundation: where mystery isn't a threat but a friend, where questions aren't punishments but invitations.

This is where mysticism offers its most profound wisdom: faith isn't assent to propositions but union with the Living God. It isn't a fortress of answers but a river of love. To reconstruct after deconstruction is to shift from defending beliefs to embodying grace.

St. John of the Cross wrote, "In the twilight of life, we will be judged by love alone."[17] The measure of mature faith isn't doctrinal precision but compassionate presence. When belief and doubt can coexist within love, you have entered what the mystics called the unitive way: the stage of faith where everything belongs, because everything is held in God.

Here, paradox becomes prayer. You can lament and adore, protest and praise, wrestle and rest: all at once. You can hold scripture not as a weapon but as a living word that reveals and unsettles. You can speak of God without pretending to have a complete understanding.

"Mature faith isn't certainty restored; it's trust rediscovered. Such faith is the humble confidence that Christ's way, truth, life, and love are enough."

This is the mature faith that rises from the ashes of deconstruction: not a return to the past, but a deeper surrender to the mystery of love.

---

[17] St. John of the Cross, *Sayings of Light and Love*, in *The Collected Works of St. John of the Cross*, Saying 64.

The Church Beyond the Wilderness

What does this mean for the church? It means that the wilderness wanderers must be welcomed, not shamed. The deconstructors aren't enemies of faith; they're often its prophets. Their questions reveal where the church has grown rigid, where theology has become ideology, where the Spirit has been domesticated.

Communities that fear deconstruction are communities that fear the Spirit's freedom. But those who listen, who create space for lament, doubt, and dialogue, will discover renewal. The church doesn't need to panic when people leave Egypt; it needs to learn how to accompany them through the desert.[18]

We must resist the temptation to force early arrival: to hand people new dogmas before they've had time to grieve the old. The Spirit's work in deconstruction is slow, holy, and often hidden. Our task isn't to hurry it but to hold space for it.

Imagine congregations where silence is honored as deeply as sermons, where confession is valued more than certainty, where art, lament, and prayer coexist as languages of faith. These would be places where exvangelicals, doubters, mystics, and pilgrims could rediscover belonging.

After the Unknowing

There comes a point in every pilgrim's journey when the cloud of unknowing begins to lift. The terrain of faith is still mysterious, but something new shines through: humility. Gratitude. A deep, steady joy untethered to emotion or doctrine.

The mystics called this *union*: not an escape from the world, but a renewed capacity to love it. After the long dark night, you return to the ordinary with transfigured sight. Washing dishes, listening to a friend, tending the wounded: all become sacraments of presence.

---

[18] Echoes the Exodus motif from Exodus 13–15, reframed for contemporary spiritual exile.

"In a culture addicted to certainty and outrage, those who've been through the humbling experience of deconstruction often become witnesses to another way: the Jesus Way of patient listening, humble truth, local service, and fearless love."

Those who emerge from deconstruction carrying this mystic awareness become healers. They speak with the honesty of doubt and the tenderness of faith reborn. They know that truth and love aren't opposites but companions. They've learned that mystery isn't the enemy of meaning but its deepest source.

In a culture addicted to certainty and outrage, such people become witnesses to another way: a way of patient listening, gentle truth, and fearless love.

The Mystical Future of Faith

The church of tomorrow may not look like the one we grew up in. It may be smaller, quieter, less triumphant; but perhaps also more beautiful.

It'll be a church marked by contemplative depth rather than institutional might. It'll value presence over performance, transformation over transaction. It'll draw from the ancient wells of mysticism to meet the modern hunger for authenticity.

Exvangelicals and deconstructing Christians may very well be the midwives of this renewal. Their questions aren't tearing down the church: they're clearing ground for a more spacious, compassionate faith to grow.

In a time when religion often speaks with the language of fear, the Spirit is teaching a new language: love that listens, hope that doubts honestly, truth that humbles, and freedom that serves.

The Invitation Beyond Certainty

Faith, at its best, isn't a fortress but a fire: not to be guarded but to be tended. When the mystic and the exvangelical meet, they recognize each other as pilgrims walking the same terrain: the terrain of trust without control.

This is the invitation: not to rebuild what has fallen, but to walk forward with bare feet on holy ground. To let God be God again. To love truth enough to let go of lies, even comforting ones. To live in the tension of not-knowing, and find that the unknowing itself is full of God.

"Both the mystic and the exvangelical walk through the wilderness, and both find that the darkness is full of God."

The deconstruction of faith and the mystical path aren't opposites: they're different names for the same transformation. Both strip us of illusion. Both lead us through the wilderness. Both end where all authentic journeys end: in love.

"The soul that walks in darkness and yet keeps walking in love has already reached the dawn." St. John of the Cross[19]

---

[19] Paraphrased from St. John of the Cross, *Dark Night of the Soul*, Book II, Chapter 21.

4. Doubt and Discipleship to Jesus: How Christian Spirituality Guides Our Way

There are nights when faith feels like silence. When prayer echoes into absence. When words once bright with certainty now taste like ash. It's tempting to think something has gone terribly wrong; that doubt is failure, that questioning means betrayal. Yet the witness of Scripture and the great Christian spiritual guides tells another story: doubt can be a form of grace.

Throughout Christian history, saints and seekers alike have discovered that the road to a deeper faith passes through the valley of unknowing. It's not a pleasant road. It's one lined with shadows and silence. But it's also the road where illusions die and love is purified. This is the paradox at the heart of Christian spirituality: that losing sight of God can sometimes be the way God draws us nearer.

The Faith That Questions

We often inherit a vision of faith as certainty: as unshakable conviction, smooth answers, or tidy theology. Yet the Bible refuses to cooperate with that definition. Abraham's faith began with leaving the familiar and walking into a land he didn't know. Job's faith howled with confusion. The psalms of lament cry out, "My God, my God, why have you forsaken me?": a prayer Jesus himself would later make his own.[20] Even John the Baptist, who once pointed to Christ as the Lamb of God, sent a question

---

[20] Psalm 22:1; Matthew 27:46.

from his prison cell: "Are you the one who is to come, or should we look for another?"

Faith, then, isn't certainty. Faith is trust in the presence of God, even when that presence feels hidden. It's the courage to keep walking when the map no longer makes sense. Doubt, far from being its opposite, is the pressure that keeps faith alive, stretching it beyond our comfort zones toward maturity.

"Doubt is the midwife of deeper trust."

When we hold our questions in the light of prayer, they can become the soil where a more authentic faith takes root. Certainty is brittle; it shatters under the weight of mystery. But trust (faith that wrestles, waits, and wonders) endures.

The Dark Night and the Fire of Love

St. John of the Cross called this transformation the dark night of the soul.[21] He didn't mean depression or the collapse of belief, but rather the experience of God removing the false supports of our spirituality (the feelings, the certainties, the familiar consolations) so that we can love God for God's own sake. In this night, the mystic learns that faith isn't a feeling but a fidelity, not light grasped but love endured.

In his poetry, John writes of the soul going out "in darkness and secure," led only by the fire burning in the heart.[22] That fire is love, and its light is enough. The darkness doesn't mean God is gone; it means God is too near, too vast, too real to be contained in our small images.

"When we can no longer see God with our eyes, we are invited to see with our hearts."

Julian of Norwich came to the same truth through her visions of divine mystery.[23] She saw both the horror of suffering and the relentless mercy of God. Her most famous words ("All shall be well, and all shall be well, and all manner of thing shall be well") were not naïve optimism.

---

[21] St. John of the Cross, *Dark Night of the Soul.*
[22] St. John of the Cross, *The Collected Works of St. John of the Cross.*
[23] Julian of Norwich, *Revelations of Divine Love.*

They were the hard-won faith of someone who had stared into the abyss and still trusted love to have the final word.

The anonymous author of The Cloud of Unknowing took this even further, teaching that we approach God not through knowledge but through love. "By love," he writes, "God may be gotten and held, but by thought never."[24] In other words, we can't think our way to God. We can only surrender.

This surrender isn't resignation but reverence. It's the humility of realizing that God is a mystery, not an equation to be solved, but a relationship to be entered.

When God Is Silent

There are seasons when God seems to disappear: when prayers feel unanswered, when the heavens are brass, when joy gives way to bewilderment. Simone Weil, the French philosopher and mystic, called this "the absence of God."[25] She believed such absence could be a form of grace: a stripping away of our self-made idols, an invitation to love God without reward. "When everything we rely on has been taken away," she wrote, "what remains is the space where God can dwell."

"Sometimes God withdraws not to punish, but to purify our love: to teach us to seek the Giver, not the gift."

Thomas Merton echoed this in the twentieth century. He saw doubt as the shadow cast by genuine faith, a sign that our relationship with God was alive, dynamic, and honest. "Faith," he wrote, "isn't a conviction that something is true, but a surrender to the One who is truth."[26]

To doubt, in this sense, is to confess that we aren't God. It's to recognize the limits of our understanding, the finitude of our grasp, the fragility of our vision. It's the soul's way of kneeling.

---

[24] Anonymous, *The Cloud of Unknowing.*
[25] Weil, *Waiting for God.*
[26] Merton, *New Seeds of Contemplation.*

The Idols That Must Fall

Much of what passes for faith in modern religion is, in truth, a craving for control. We prefer a domesticated deity who always agrees with our opinions and blesses our agendas. But the living God can't be contained by our categories.

The Christian spiritual writers warn that before we find the true God, we must let the false gods die: the gods of certainty, nationalism, tribal identity, and fear. These idols promise security but deliver prisons. When doubt shatters them, it's not destruction but liberation.

Jesus himself overturned the idols of his age: the idol of purity that excluded, the idol of empire that oppressed, the idol of religious superiority that condemned. His way isn't about possessing truth but embodying it in love. The disciple who doubts yet still follows, still serves, still loves: is closer to the kingdom than the one who boasts of certainty but lacks compassion.

"The church's renewal will come not from louder certainties, but from deeper humility: when we trust love more than we fear mystery."

Doubt as Solidarity

To doubt is also to join the company of saints who have known the silence of God. Jesus himself entered that silence. On the cross, he cried out, "My God, my God, why have you forsaken me?" That lament wasn't unbelief; it was the deepest form of faith: the refusal to let go of God even when God seemed absent.

Every person who doubts stands, in that moment, in the shadow of the cross. And every cry of confusion is heard by the One who also cried. In this sense, doubt can be an act of solidarity: with Christ, and with every suffering soul who has ever felt abandoned or unsure.

The resurrection doesn't erase that darkness; it transfigures it. When the risen Jesus appeared to Thomas, he didn't scold him for doubting. He invited him to touch his wounds. Genuine faith doesn't avoid the wounds; it learns to find God in them.

From Deconstruction to Resurrection

Many today describe themselves as "deconstructing" their faith. They're peeling back layers of inherited theology, questioning institutions that have wounded, unlearning versions of God that no longer hold. This process can feel lonely, even dangerous. But it can also be holy.

Every generation must, in its own way, rediscover the gospel beneath the rubble of religion. Deconstruction, if it leads to truth and love, isn't destruction but resurrection.

The Exodus story offers a mirror for this moment. Israel left Egypt not because they had lost faith, but because they were following a deeper call. The desert felt like death, yet it was the space where new faith was born. The same Spirit that led Jesus into the wilderness still leads us there: not to abandon us, but to teach us trust.

For those walking this wilderness of doubt: don't be afraid. God isn't offended by your questions. The divine presence is large enough to hold your confusion, your grief, your anger. Sometimes God hides not to torment us, but to draw us into honesty: to invite a relationship not built on fear, but on freedom.

Learning to Live the Questions

Rainer Maria Rilke once wrote: "Be patient toward all that is unsolved in your heart and try to love the questions themselves."[27] That's a profoundly Christian invitation. Discipleship to Jesus doesn't mean having all the answers; it means walking with the Answer even when we don't understand the path.

To follow Jesus is to live within holy tension: between faith and doubt, presence and absence, light and shadow. The Christian spiritual writers teach us that faith grows best when we no longer rely on sight. As Paul wrote, "We walk by faith, not by sight."[28]

---

[27] Rilke, *Letters to a Young Poet.*
[28] 2 Corinthians 5:7.

This walking faith is slow, honest, and free. It doesn't shy away from hard truths about the world: injustice, suffering, and the failures of the church. It looks them in the eye, laments them, and still chooses love.

In our time of disillusionment, the invitation isn't to abandon faith, but to purify it; to let it burn away what is false so that what remains is real.

Silence, Mystery, and the Presence That Holds

There's a line in The Cloud of Unknowing that reads, "For He may well be loved, but not thought." That is the task of the contemplative (and of every disciple in doubt) to love what can't be grasped.

In the silence of prayer, beyond concepts and doctrines, we sometimes glimpse what we can't say: the gentle nearness of a Presence that holds all things. This isn't the end of questioning, but the peace that allows questioning to continue without despair.

When you no longer know how to pray, sit in silence. When you can't say "I believe," whisper "I long to believe." Grace will meet you there. For grace isn't found in certainty, but in the willingness to remain open.

"Faith begins not in knowing, but in staying: in choosing to remain before the mystery long enough for love to speak."

The Return to Simplicity

After the long night, something remarkable happens. The soul emerges quieter, humbler, freer. The faith that once demanded answers becomes content with presence. The believer who once argued theology now simply loves.

This is the fruit of doubt transformed by grace: compassion. Those who have walked through unknowing rarely judge others who struggle. They've seen too much of their own fragility. They've learned that mercy is truer than dogma.

When Thomas finally touched the wounds of Christ, he didn't deliver a sermon. He simply said, "My Lord and my God."That's where mature faith leads, not to mastery, but to wonder.

A Church That Can Hold Questions

For the church, the challenge is clear: will we be a community where people can doubt safely? Where questions aren't silenced but honored as part of the journey?

If we can recover the contemplative heart of the faith, we might rediscover how to hold space for seekers and skeptics alike. Louder proclamations of certainty won't renew the church's witness to Christ, but by deeper practices of love: by communities that embody patience, hospitality, and listening.

The Christian spiritual writers remind us that the gospel isn't an argument to win, but a mystery to enter. The church must become again a school of the Spirit, where hearts learn the language of love more than the language of fear.

The Dawn Beyond the Darkness

At the end of Dark Night of the Soul, St. John of the Cross describes the dawn after the long night.[29] The soul, purified of illusion, finally rests in the gentle presence of God. He writes, "The soul that walks in darkness and yet keeps walking in love has already reached the dawn."

That's the promise for those who doubt yet keep walking. You may feel lost, but love is leading you. Every honest question, every broken prayer, every long silence may be preparing you for the dawn.

And when the dawn comes, you'll find that the God you thought you'd lost was walking beside you all along.

"Faith isn't the absence of doubt; it's the courage to love through the doubt, trusting that grace still has the last word."

---

[29] St. John of the Cross, *Dark Night of the Soul.*

A Prayer for Those Who Doubt

O Christ of the wilderness,
You who walked in silence and wrestled with despair,
     hold close all who wander through the shadows of doubt.
Let them know they're not lost, only being led deeper.
Strip away our idols, our fears, our false certainties,
     until all that remains is love.
Teach us to rest not in clarity, but in communion.
And when the night feels endless,
     whisper your word of promise:
     "All shall be well."
Amen.

Doubt is the fire that can forge faith. To follow Jesus is to step into the mystery, to walk by faith through the night, and to find that even in our unknowing, God's love remains: patient, tender, and endlessly new.

PART II — CHRIST, SCRIPTURE, AND DISCERNMENT: DEPTH FOR A FRACTURED AGE

Part II examines how Scripture, discernment, and Christ-shaped practices cut through our idols and illusions, calling us into a deeper, wiser, more cruciform discipleship that resists both cultural captivity and shallow religion.

5. How the Bible Shapes Christian Discipleship and Spirituality

There are few things more radical than believing that the living God speaks: still, now, through words on a page. Compared with the views of our age, it's an astonishing conviction to believe that these words in Scripture, ancient yet alive, can pierce the noise of history and the chatter of our minds to reveal truth that heals, convicts, and remakes the world. For Christians, the Bible isn't merely a sacred text among others. It's the inspired witness to God's self-revelation in Jesus Christ: the Word through whom all words find their meaning.

The Bible isn't a weapon. It's not a political tool, nor a manual for domination. It's the story of divine love breaking into human history: the record of God's relentless pursuit of creation, culminating in Christ, who is both the center and the key. To read it rightly is to listen for the heartbeat of grace. To live by it is to be shaped into the likeness of the One who is Love.

> *"Too often, we're tempted to use the Bible as a weapon, but we shouldn't treat the Bible that way. The Bible is the story of divine love breaking into human history: culminating in Christ, who is both the center and the key."*

Scripture as Living Word

When we say the Bible is the Word of God, we mean something astonishing: that through these words the Spirit still speaks. The same breath that moved over the waters in Genesis, the same voice that called prophets to justice and apostles to mission, now stirs in the hearts of readers who open the text in faith.

Scripture isn't a static record of what God *once said*. It's a living conversation between God and God's people. The Word that became flesh continues to become voice through the pages of Scripture: beckoning, confronting, comforting, loving, and commissioning.

This means that reading the Bible is never a neutral act. It's an encounter. The text reads us as much as we read it. It exposes our idols and illusions. It reveals both the glory and the poverty of the human heart. The Spirit meets us in its pages not to flatter but to transform: to turn hearers into doers, believers into disciples, and readers into witnesses.

> *"Reading Scripture is never neutral; it's an encounter where the text reads us, exposes our idols, and turns hearers into doers."*

"Your word is a lamp to my feet and a light to my path" (Psalm 119:105). The psalmist's words remind us that Scripture isn't a floodlight that removes all mystery. It's a lamp: a humble flame that illuminates just enough for the next faithful step. The Bible guides not by giving us control, but by calling us into trust.

The Authority of Love

To say that the Bible is the supreme and sufficient authority for faith and life doesn't mean it's a rigid rulebook. It means that all claims to truth, all doctrines, all moral decisions, all spiritual experiences must ultimately be tested by the story of God revealed in Scripture and brought to fulfillment in Christ.

But biblical authority is never authoritarian. It's the authority of love: an authority that liberates rather than constrains. The authority of Scripture doesn't crush human conscience; it awakens it. It doesn't silence honest questioning; it sanctifies it.

Every true reading of Scripture leads us deeper into the mind of Christ, who is the final Word of God. If our interpretations breed cruelty, exclusion, or arrogance, they've missed the Spirit's intent. "The letter kills, but the Spirit gives life" (2 Corinthians 3:6). The authority of the Bible isn't about control but transformation: shaping us into a people whose lives reflect the love of God for the world.[30]

To trust Scripture as authoritative is to submit our imagination to its story, allowing it to dismantle false narratives of power and pride. It means letting the Sermon on the Mount interpret our politics, letting the prophets shape our economics, letting the Gospels reorder our priorities.

"Too many treat biblical authority as control. But, following the Way of Jesus means viewing biblical authority as cruciform love: an authority that liberates the conscience and forms us into the mind and image of Jesus Christ."

Authority, in biblical terms, means the power to give life. And Scripture, when read in the Spirit, does just that: it breathes life into weary bones and calls the church to rise.

The Freedom of Conscience and the Fellowship of Interpretation

Every believer is called to read and discern the Word of God. There are no spiritual elites who monopolize interpretation. The Reformers' conviction that all believers share a "priesthood" wasn't an attack on scholarship or tradition; it was an affirmation that the Spirit speaks to all within the fellowship of faith.[31]

To read Scripture "in the freedom of conscience" means that each follower of Jesus must engage it personally, responsibly, and prayerfully, willing to be shaped and corrected. But such freedom is never isolation. The same Spirit who illumines individual minds binds the community together. The church is the interpretive home of the Word, the space where believers discern truth not as private consumers but as a body seeking wisdom together.

---

[30] Augustine, *On Christian Doctrine*, 1.36–40.
[31] Luther, *To the Christian Nobility.*

The Bible is best read not in echo chambers but around tables: where diverse voices wrestle, question, and listen. Faithful interpretation requires humility: the willingness to be taught by the global and historical church, by the poor and the marginalized, by those whose experiences differ from our own.

The truth of Scripture isn't fragile. It doesn't need to be protected from scrutiny. It needs to be practiced in love.

The Bible's Rhythm: From Hearing to Doing

The Bible isn't meant to be admired from afar; it's meant to be lived. In both Testaments, the pattern is clear: God speaks, people act. The Word calls us to obedience, not as coercion but as participation in divine life. When Jesus tells the parable of the wise and foolish builders, he draws the line not between those who *hear* his words and those who don't, but between those who hear *and do* them (Matthew 7:24–27). The Word of God creates disciples who embody what they hear.

Reading Scripture prayerfully means letting it form habits of mercy, justice, and humility. Reading it contextually means attending to its world so we can rightly interpret it in ours: hearing it first in the voice of ancient Israel, then through the Word made flesh, and finally in the chorus of witnesses who have lived its truth.

Reading it obediently means more than just moral compliance. It means surrender. It means saying, with Mary, "Let it be to me according to your word" (Luke 1:38). The goal isn't mastery of the text; it's the transformation of the heart.

The Bible as a Prophetic Mirror

When Scripture is read rightly, it turns our gaze outward as much as inward. It reveals the idols of our age: greed disguised as freedom, nationalism disguised as faith, violence disguised as justice.

The prophets understood that to know the Word of God is to be summoned into history: to confront oppression, to defend those experiencing poverty, and to seek peace. Isaiah's vision of God's Word going forth like rain that "doesn't return empty" (Isaiah 55:11) isn't about private spirituality alone. It's about a Word that transforms economies, politics, and human hearts.

Jesus, steeped in Scripture, embodied this prophetic vocation. He announced good news to people experiencing poverty, freedom to captives, and sight to people who are blind. Every word he spoke was Scripture fulfilled, and every silence was Scripture waiting to be revealed.

To follow Jesus is to let that same Word shape our moral imagination. It means reading the Bible with the eyes of the crucified: seeing the world from below, from the perspective of those who suffer. When we read Scripture this way, it becomes not an instrument of dominance but a summons to solidarity.

"Isn't my word like fire," declares the Lord, "and like a hammer that breaks a rock in pieces?" (Jeremiah 23:29). The Bible burns away illusions. It breaks the hardness of heart that justifies injustice. Yet it also kindles hope: the fire that warms a world grown cold.

The Bible Points Beyond Itself to Christ

If the Bible is the Word of God, then Jesus Christ is its grammar and syntax. Every story finds its coherence in him. He's the thread that runs from Genesis to Revelation, the living exegesis of divine love.

The Bible points beyond itself. Its words aren't an end, but a way: a lamp leading us to the living Word who speaks them. When we read Scripture apart from Christ, it becomes brittle and weaponized. But when we read through the lens of his life, death, and resurrection, every command becomes an invitation to love.

Jesus himself modeled this hermeneutic. When he walked with the disciples on the road to Emmaus, "beginning with Moses and all the Prophets, he explained to them what was said in all the Scriptures concerning himself" (Luke 24:27). The result wasn't intellectual agreement: it was burning hearts and open eyes. That's the mark of Spirit-filled reading: not more certainty, but more wonder.

Every true interpretation leads us deeper into the mystery of the crucified and risen Christ. Every false interpretation forgets him.

Christ at the Center: The Logic of Redemption and Revelation

The logic of Christianity begins and ends with Christ. The gospel's claim isn't one truth among many, but *the* truth: that in Jesus of Nazareth, God has acted once and for all to reconcile creation to the Creator. There's no salvation outside of him, not because divine love is narrow, but because divine love has become personal. "No one comes to God except through me," Jesus said, not as a threat, but as an invitation to communion (John 14:6). In him, the fullness of God dwells bodily; in him, the human story meets its healing and its home. To confess Christ as Lord is to affirm that every path to truth, justice, mercy, reconciliation, healing, salvation, and peace ultimately finds its meaning in the One who is Truth itself.

> *"If Christ is the center, every true interpretation moves toward reconciliation. If our interpretation and application of the Bible breeds cruelty or pride, it's missed the Spirit's intent."*

This centrality of Christ shapes how we read and live the Scriptures. The Bible is a unified witness pointing toward the living Word. Every page, law, lament, poem, song, epistle, narrative, and prophecy finds its fulfillment in him. To read the Bible rightly is to read it through the cross and resurrection: to see its ultimate trajectory as reconciliation, not condemnation. When Christ is the center, interpretation becomes an act of discipleship: we discern together what faithfulness to him looks like in our time. His love becomes the hermeneutic through which we judge every doctrine, ethic, and public action. In a world prone to using Scripture for division or domination, the church is called to read the Word in the Spirit of Christ: to apply it in ways that heal, humanize, and proclaim the reconciling love that holds the cosmos together.

The Bible and the Contemplative Life

If Scripture shapes discipleship, it must also shape our prayer. The contemplative tradition teaches that reading the Bible isn't about acquiring information, but about transforming. *Lectio divina* (the ancient practice of sacred reading) invites us to slow down, to listen, to allow the Word to descend from the mind to the heart.[32]

We read, meditate, pray, and rest, not to master the text but to be mastered by it. The Word becomes flesh in us as we sit in silence, allowing divine truth to permeate our being (John 1:5 and 14).

In a world addicted to speed and slogans, contemplative reading is an act of resistance. It reclaims speech as sacred and silence as fertile. It reminds us that revelation isn't grasped by argument but received by love.

To read the Bible contemplatively is to hear God's whisper amid the noise of empires. It's to let Scripture train our attention until we can recognize the voice of Christ in the cry of the poor, the beauty of creation, and the quiet ache of our own hearts.

---

[32] Guigo II, *The Ladder of Monks and Twelve Meditations.*

The Bible and the Life of the Church

Scripture doesn't form solitary spiritual leaders only: it forms a people. From Israel gathered at Sinai to the church gathered around Word and Table, the Bible creates community.

Every time believers read Scripture together, something sacramental occurs: the Spirit joins lives into a single story. Across languages, centuries, and continents, the Bible becomes our shared songbook. It gives us a grammar of hope when our own words fail.

When the early church heard the Scriptures read aloud, they responded not with applause or critique but with obedience. They believed the Word wasn't only to be heard but also to be enacted. Their communal reading led to a shared life: one of generosity, forgiveness, and radical hospitality.

That's the test of biblical spirituality: not how much we know, but how well we love. Scripture's authority is vindicated when it produces communities of compassion that embody God's reign.

Reading the Bible in a Wounded World

Today, the Bible is often co-opted to justify nationalism, misogyny, exclusion, and greed. It's used to wound rather than heal. But the same text, when read in the Spirit of Christ, can dismantle these distortions.

To reclaim the Bible for discipleship, we must return to its prophetic and pastoral roots. The Word of God calls us not to power but to servanthood, not to certainty but to compassion. It draws us into solidarity with the oppressed, challenges our privilege, and reminds us that love of God is inseparable from love of neighbor.

Reading the Bible faithfully in this age of polarization means resisting the temptation to use it as a weapon in tribal battles. It means reading it as a pilgrim, not a gatekeeper. The Word was never given to justify our fears; it was given to set us free.

In a time when truth is cheap and outrage sells, the church's witness will depend on how we embody the Word, not in slogans, but in lives that echo its melody: mercy, justice, humility, and hope.

The Word That Became Flesh, Again

At the heart of Christian discipleship is imitation: becoming like the One we follow. The Bible is the Spirit's primary tool for this formation. But the end of Bible reading is never mere knowledge; it's Christlikeness.

When Scripture takes root in us, it begins to incarnate again. The Word becomes flesh in our speech, our choices, our compassion. Our communities become living commentaries: interpretations written not with ink, but with lives of grace.

To live biblically, then, is to let the story of God rewrite our own. It's to see every stranger as a neighbor, every enemy as a potential sibling, every act of mercy as Scripture fulfilled.

A Word for Our Time

The Bible's relevance isn't that it answers every modern question; it's that it draws us into a story big enough to hold every question. Its truth isn't formulaic but relational. It doesn't give us certainty; it gives us communion.

Our task isn't to defend the Bible as if it were fragile, but to let it defend the world from despair. In its pages, we hear again the ancient, defiant hope: that light shines in the darkness, and the darkness can't overcome it.

When we open Scripture, we open the door to that light. We listen for the voice that speaks creation into being, justice into chaos, peace into violence. And if we listen long enough, that voice begins to shape us until our own speech becomes creative, truthful, and kind.

A Prayer for the Word to Take Flesh Again

O God who speaks still,
        teach us to hear your Word amid the noise of our time.
Strip away our idols of certainty and control.
Let your Scriptures burn in us as fire, not a weapon.
Turn our reading into repentance, our knowledge into love.
Make us a people who don't merely quote your Word,
        but embody it;
                in justice that rolls down like water,
                in mercy that never ends,
                in faith that walks humbly with you.
Let your Word once more become flesh among us,
        and let the world see in your people
        the living proof that your story is still being told.
Amen.

6. Keeping Christ at the Center: Resisting Idolatry in an Age of Distraction

There's a tragedy unfolding in many corners of the church today. It isn't loud enough to make headlines. It doesn't announce itself with scandal or collapse. Instead, it moves like a subtle fog through sanctuaries and institutions, soft enough that few notice the drift. It begins whenever something good, something noble, helpful, even beautiful, slowly becomes ultimate. Whenever a community forgets that Christ is the axis on which all creation turns, and begins to revolve around something else.

"Idolatry rarely shouts; it drifts in to our hearts, asking only that we centre our lives on something almost, but not quite, Jesus Christ."

Idolatry isn't only the worship of false gods. It's also the slow surrender of the heart to lesser lights. It's the ease with which we centre our communities on the wrong thing, on ideology, personality, nostalgia, novelty, mysticism, doctrine, or tribal belonging, and only later realise that Christ has become a supporting character in a story meant to be shaped entirely by Christ's presence and rule.

This problem is a shared vulnerability across the Christian household. Conservatives and progressives, liturgical communities and charismatic movements, traditional churches and experimental ones, every tradition has its temptations and its treasured idols. The forms differ, but the pattern is the same: when we take something good and treat it as the organising force of our life together, it begins to compete with the One who alone can hold the whole.

So this is a call, not to shame or scold, but to awaken. To remember what's true. To clear the fog and see again the crucified and risen Christ, whose beauty and authority alone can hold the church in unity, humility, holiness, and hope.

The church doesn't need more strategies or better optics. It needs to recover its centre. It needs to relearn the ancient posture of surrender, turning its face toward Christ until all the counterfeit lights fade to their proper size.

What follows is an invitation to examine the things churches often elevate to the status of idols, to reflect on why Christ's lordship is essential, and to imagine the practices that help communities keep Christ as the blazing centre of their life together.

The Things We Turn Into Idols

If idolatry were obvious, we'd resist it. But it's subtle because it often hides beneath good intentions or cherished commitments. Here are the things Christians commonly elevate until they threaten to replace Christ's centrality.

"The danger isn't that we worship obvious false gods, but that we elevate good things until they become ultimate things."

1. Political or cultural ideology

Left or right, revolutionary or preservationist, any ideology can become a functional savior. When our politics define our theology instead of the other way around, we've enthroned a rival lord.

2. Tradition or innovation

Some communities cling to what's ancient; others chase everything new. Christ can be lost in both nostalgia and novelty when either becomes the measure of truth or faithfulness.

3. Institutional reputation and survival

When protecting the institution becomes more important than truth, repentance, justice, or vulnerability, the institution becomes an idol dressed in religious language.

4. Doctrinal or moral superiority

Right belief and right living matter profoundly, but when they become badges of spiritual achievement, they choke out humility and grace.

5. Charismatic leaders and personalities

When communities organise themselves around gifts rather than Christ, they tether themselves to clay rather than to glory.

6. Nationalism, tribal loyalty, or cultural identity

Any identity marker that demands ultimate allegiance becomes a competitor with Christ's kingdom.

7. Success, growth, and measurable impact

Numbers, influence, and achievement can masquerade as faithfulness even as they hollow out a community's soul.

8. Comfort, stability, and control

Churches often cling to predictability and self-protection at the expense of discernment and obedience. Fear of loss becomes an idol.

9. Social justice or evangelism elevated as the whole gospel

Both are essential dimensions of Christian life, but when either becomes totalising, the gospel shrinks into ideology or activism unmoored from grace.

10. Scripture as an end rather than a witness

The Bible is sacred, but it points beyond itself. When the text replaces encounter with the living Christ, revelation becomes an idol.

11. Spiritual experiences and emotional highs

Mystical depth, charismatic wonder, and contemplative sweetness, each beautiful in its place, can become idols when they define what counts as "real" spirituality.

12. Purity codes or self-defined liberation

Whether rooted in conservative moral categories or progressive ethical visions, purity and liberation can eclipse the transforming holiness of Christ.

13. Community belonging elevated above truthfulness

A beloved community can become a soft idol when belonging means never challenging one another toward holiness and surrender.

14. Programs, methods, and ecclesial systems

Churches often rely more on the machinery of ministry than on the presence of Christ.

15. Suffering, activism, or service as identity

When identity rests in how much we sacrifice or accomplish, self-justification replaces grace.

These idols aren't always consciously chosen. They're usually inherited, absorbed, or assumed. They often arise from longing for clarity, safety, relevance, righteousness, or belonging. But when they become central, they distort the church's imagination and mis-form its witness.

"When Jesus Christ ceases to be the centre, something else always rushes in to take that place, and it never carries life."

Why Idolatry Is So Dangerous, And Why Christ's Lordship Matters

Idolatry is a spiritual disfiguration. It changes not just what we believe but who we become. And it does so by replacing the living centre with something that can't carry the weight of a community's hopes, fears, and mission.

Idolatry deforms our imagination.

Whatever sits at the centre of a church shapes how that church thinks, dreams, prays, and loves. If ideology sits at the centre, communities become combative. If stability controls the center, communities become rigid. If success defines the centre, communities become anxious and performative.

But when Christ is central, imagination is formed by the cross's humility and the resurrection's hope. The community becomes spacious, generous, courageous, and rooted.

Idolatry reshapes desire.

Idols offer an illusion of control. They give a sense of clarity: "If we cling to this, all will be well." But they demand constant feeding and attention. They generate anxiety. They ask us to protect them. They train us to fear the loss of what we've elevated.

Christ's lordship does the opposite. Christ frees communities from fear. Christ invites them to trust, to surrender, to rest in a love that doesn't need to be defended.

Idolatry fractures community.

When something other than Christ is central, factions form around that thing. The church becomes a battlefield of camps, each guarding its version of righteousness or purity. Tribal belonging overrides unity. Fear overrides love.

But when Christ is central, walls fall. People learn to listen across differences. Commitment to humility, repentance, and reconciliation becomes part of the community's DNA.

Idolatry compromises mission.

A church centred on anything other than Christ becomes conformed to the patterns of its surrounding culture. It absorbs the anxieties, hostilities, and categories of its age. Its witness dims.

A Christ-centred community remains rooted in something deeper and older, something unshakeable, holy, alive. It resists the cultural tides not with contempt but with Christ-shaped compassion.

Ultimately, idols can't save.

They can't heal wounds or break chains. They can't forgive, restore, or renew. They offer the illusion of power but no transformation.

Only Christ can hold the human heart. Only Christ can reconcile enemies, restore communities,. breathe hope into despair, and lead us into holiness. Only Christ is the true centre.

To say Christ is Lord is to proclaim the most profound truth of the universe: that all things find their meaning, coherence, and future in Christ alone.

The Psychology of Drift, How Good Things Become Gods

A community rarely becomes idolatrous through conscious rebellion. It happens through drift, a subtle, almost imperceptible turning of attention.

It happens when a community begins to fear loss more than it trusts Christ.

It happens when habits formed by culture slowly replace habits formed by prayer.

It happens when the urgency of the moment overwhelms the eternal call to faithfulness.

It happens when a church is shaped more by scarcity than by abundance, more by anxiety than by hope.

"Idols promise control, clarity, individuality, freedom, and belonging, but they always take more from us than they give."

Idolatry is rarely about the idol itself. It's about the need beneath the idol, the longing for stability, belonging, clarity, or control. Only Christ can address that need without distorting the soul. Every other source of security becomes a trap.

The church needs courage to confront this drift, not with condemnation but with gentle clarity. Communities must cultivate the humility to say: "Something noble has taken a place it was never meant to hold. We must return."

"Communities don't keep Christ central through slogans but through habits that re-shape desire and re-train the heart."

And returning is always possible. Christ's mercy makes restoration not only achievable but joyful.

Keeping Christ Central: The Practices That Shape a Faithful Community

Christ remains central not through slogans but through practices, habits of life that continually reorient the heart and refocus the imagination.

Here are some of the essential practices that help a community keep Christ enthroned at the center:

1. The practice of shared repentance

Christian community begins where pride ends. Repentance is revelation, a return to clarity. A Christ-centred church confesses its temptations, its idols, its distortions. It tells the truth. It refuses self-justification. It lets humility become its deepest breath.

2. The practice of contemplative stillness

Silence unmakes the idols we didn't know we worshiped. It creates space where the Spirit dismantles illusions and awakens desire for Christ. A quieted heart becomes fertile soil for Christ's voice.

3. The practice of Scripture as encounter

A Christ-centered church reads Scripture not as a weapon or rulebook but as a meeting place, a living Word that reveals the One who speaks through it. The Bible is no longer the centre, but the window to the centre.

4. The practice of worship that awakens wonder

Worship rooted in awe and humility pulls the church back into alignment with Christ's glory. It reminds the community of the vastness of grace and the smallness of everything else.

5. The practice of community that crosses boundaries

A Christ-centred community intentionally resists tribal formation. It welcomes the stranger. It cultivates friendships across differences. It refuses the illusion that sameness is holiness.

6. The practice of sacrificial hospitality

Hospitality opens the door to the presence of Christ hidden in the vulnerable, the outsider, the forgotten. It forms the church into a people whose centre is compassion rather than self-protection.

7. The practice of sabbath and simplicity

Sabbath unmasks the idolatry of productivity. Simplicity unmasks the idolatry of accumulation. Together, they create space for Christ to reorder the heart.

8. The practice of communal discernment

Christ is central when communities pray, listen, reflect, and decide together, seeking not victory but truth, not efficiency but wisdom, not control but surrender.

9. The practice of peacemaking

Christ's lordship is revealed through communities that refuse vengeance, nurture reconciliation, seek justice with tenderness, and love enemies with costly fidelity.

10. The practice of hope

Hope keeps Christ at the centre because it remembers that the future belongs not to our idols but to the One who has overcome death. Hope sets the heart free from fear.

> *"Silence, solitude, prayer, and Scripture unmask the idols we didn't know we trusted and opens the soul to the glorious, holy, loving, presence we can no longer ignore."*

Signs a Church Is Re-Centering on Christ

Every church needs markers, compass points that reveal whether Christ is truly at the centre. These signs aren't flashy or impressive; they're quiet and costly.

A Christ-centered church:
- tells the truth about itself,
- leans toward repentance rather than defensiveness,
- embraces humility rather than triumphalism,
- cultivates a spirit of prayer rather than strategy alone,
- listens before speaking,
- extends mercy before judgment,
- forms disciples before consumers,
- welcomes difference without losing conviction,
- loves enemies rather than imitating culture's rage,
- seeks justice without losing tenderness,

- adores Christ above every earthly loyalty.

"A Christ-centred church is marked not by triumph but by tenderness, not by certainty but by humility, not by performance but by presence, not by self-righteous judgementalism but by love."

When these qualities begin to grow, even in small, fragile ways, the church is becoming itself again.

The Joy and Freedom of Christ-Centred Living

This entire conversation isn't about moralising or burdening weary communities with more tasks. It's about liberation. It's about joy.

A Christ-centred church is free, free from fear, free from tribal captivity, free from anxiety about success or failure. It no longer needs to protect its idols or defend its illusions. It lives from the deep well of Christ's mercy and truth.

A Christ-centred community becomes a sign of another world breaking into this one:

A world where enemies are reconciled.

A world where holiness and compassion dance together.

A world where honesty is normal and pretence is unnecessary.

A world where suffering is met with tenderness.

A world where the humble are lifted up, and the proud are invited into repentance.

A world where hope refuses to die.

"Christ dismantles our idols without dismantling us: this is the mercy that makes transformation possible."

When Christ is at the centre, the church pours out beauty instead of fear, healing instead of defensiveness, generosity instead of scarcity, courage instead of compromise.

Christ alone is large enough to hold all our longing. Christ alone is gentle enough to heal our wounds. Christ alone is strong enough to break our idols without breaking us.

A Final Word

The church stands at a crossroads in this generation. The temptation toward idolatry is immense, not because the church has grown weak, but because the culture is loud. The idols of this age are persuasive. They promise clarity, security, belonging, identity, and power.

But there is another way.

A way that begins in humility.

A way that walks the path of the cross.

A way that burns with resurrection hope.

A way that refuses every rival centre.

A way that makes the love of Christ the gravitational force drawing all things together.

This is the way the church must walk, again and again, generation after generation. The way of surrender. The way of truth. The way of love.

And whenever the church returns to Christ as the center, the world sees not an institution fighting for relevance, but a people shining with the beauty of the One who called them from darkness into light.

May Christ be the centre.

May Christ be the beginning and the end.

"When Christ is the centre, the church becomes a living sign of the world God is bringing to birth."

May Christ, in all Christ's glory, humility, and love, draw us back from our idols and shape us into a people who look, act, live, and hope like Christ.

7. Whistle-Blowing Glorifies Christ: Challenging Narcissistic Leaders and Toxic Cultures

The church needs whistle-blowers who speak up to power and challenge abusive behaviour. Whistleblowing often glorifies Jesus Christ. Christian whistle-blowers challenge narcissistic leaders and toxic cultures and invite us to be the church truly.

Narcissistic Leaders

When I listen to the stories of abuse, I notice two things: narcissistic leadership and toxic cultures.

Abusive leaders are often narcissistic. They reject critical feedback and demand absolute loyalty. Let's look at some examples of this kind of leadership.

John is the senior pastor of a church, and he loves to control its vision and direction. He also loves being in the limelight and in front of a camera. One day, John decides that the church needs a compelling public vision to attract new members. He's sure the best way to do this is to post videos everywhere on social media. Without consulting anyone, John develops a vision and mission statement over a couple of days, expecting everyone to follow them. He then films himself enthusiastically talking about this vision and posts the videos on social media.

When a few members of John's church leadership team see these videos posted all over social media, they are very concerned. They can't see how the vision looks anything like their church, or if it's the right one for their church. They don't understand why no one was consulted before this went public. So, they decide together that they need to talk with John about this.

When they raise the matter with John, he's immediately defensive and angry. How dare they question this "biblical" vision? Why are they so disloyal? Can't they see that he only did this for the good of the church? Why do they constantly undermine him and ask negative questions? John is so angry and hurt that he shuts down the conversation and tells them not to talk to anyone else about their concerns. To do so would be disloyal and disobedient to God's instructions to honour leaders! Talking about these things would hinder God's work and cause future problems. If they were truly following Jesus, then they would support, honour, and praise God's leaders.

A few months later, John removes these members from his church leadership team. He's convinced he's doing the right thing. There is no place in God's church for disloyalty, negativity, and a critical spirit.

Sadly, these stories are familiar in churches. As Michael Jensen says, we need people who challenge such leaders and refuse to give uncritical loyalty. We need whistle-blowers who, like the prophet Nathan, challenge powerful and influential leaders when necessary.

Toxic Cultures

Abusive leadership often happens within toxic cultures. When you listen to people who've come out of abusive churches or organisations, they tell you that the system was toxic. The organisation behaved in a damaging way, and we can't lay all the blame at the feet of one leader.

Let's pick up where we left off on the story of John and his church. A couple of years after our first story, Anthony, one of John's associate pastors, questions how John treats people. Anthony tries to talk with John about how John shuts down and attacks the character of anyone who expresses a different view or asks questions about what John is doing.

John is hurt and furious. How dare Anthony question his behaviour? Why did he ever employ an associate pastor who is so disloyal and critical? John tells Anthony that this behaviour will be addressed in his performance review and that if Anthony raises such issues again, his employment contract won't be renewed.

But Anthony decides that he can't ignore what's going on. Too many lives are being damaged. So, after conversations with his mentor and his wife, Anthony writes a respectful letter to the church Board, asking them to help, intervene, and address this issue. Anthony points out that many people in the congregation are talking about John's abusive leadership in private, but are afraid of the consequences of speaking up publicly.

But the Board's reaction isn't what Anthony expected. One month later, the Board demanded that Anthony meet with them. At the meeting, they tell Anthony that, after much prayer, they've agreed that they can't have someone on the pastoral team who is undermining John and stirring up trouble.

The Board gives Anthony a letter of termination and tells him they'll provide him with two months' pay plus an additional $40,000, but first he must sign an NDA (a non-disclosure/non-disparagement agreement). Anthony is also told he must sign a Deed of Release that prevents him from ever seeking damages through Fair Work or a court for the way he has been unfairly treated.

Anthony signs these documents because he's now lost his job, and he's afraid he won't be able to feed his family or send his children to school without this money. Anthony feels traumatised by the experience and walks away from pastoral ministry.

John's abusive, narcissistic, controlling leadership continues. The toxic culture of the Board and congregation supports this leadership style. This church culture defends John at all costs, punishes those who speak up, and rewards silence and submission. Such toxic cultures nurture and protect narcissistic leadership and reward uncritical loyalty.

Narcissistic Leaders Need To Be Challenged

I recently listened to a radio program on leadership that addressed narcissistic leadership. Narcissists tend to do four things when people challenge their decisions or actions. First, they deny they've done anything wrong. Then, they blame others for the situation. Then, they feel indignant and angry that they've been challenged or criticised. Narcissistic leaders work assiduously to shore up perceived allies and isolate the complainant through carefully distributed character attacks. Finally, they retaliate – they perceive all critical feedback as a personal attack, and they'll always retaliate.

Christian narcissists usually have two faces. The first is the moral, spiritual, and angelic face they show the world. The other is the controlling, uncompassionate, and abusive face they show their spouse, family, and those who are closest to them. They break the spirit of those around them, gaslighting, blaming, and manipulating people around them, and creating a position where they are no longer accountable or questioned. Narcissistic leaders treat people as tools for their agendas, edifices, and egos. They view their closest allies (and supporters) with private condescension and as disposable items. That's until those persons challenge them; then their behaviour becomes vicious and unforgiving.

Whether narcissists get away with their denial, blaming, anger, and irrational retaliations depends on the strength of will and conviction of those around them. The problem is that people around these narcissistic leaders have often been gaslighted and bullied to the extent that they have no will or conviction left. So, whether people challenge the narcissist usually depends on checks and balances outside the organisation. There must be a mandate for regular, independent leadership 360s. There must also be external leaders available who have the power and will to act when damaging leadership behaviour is identified.

In my experience, it's often the "little people" who speak to power and act with extraordinary courage and fortitude, and then, usually, pay a heavy price. The higher-profile, more senior leaders often stay silent, more interested in protecting their jobs, roles, and status. (When they do speak up, it's usually because people have finally stopped ignoring the voices of the "little people," who have paid a heavy price. So, taking action now looks more virtuous, and the cost is lower).

Narcissistic, toxic, controlling leaders always demand loyalty (and they narrowly define loyalty). They then act like victims when people challenge them. In a narcissist's mind, they are always heroes or victims, but never perpetrators. This mindset is one of the reasons they feel so offended by whistle-blowers, and seek to slander the character of truth-tellers, and fight against truth-telling with such sincerity and conviction. They rarely see the damage they do to others, but always focus on the hurt they feel themselves.

Different leadership types handle shame differently. A narcissistic leader deals with shame by refusing to admit to themselves or anyone else that they've done anything wrong. They build a story for themselves and others that absolves them from guilt and saves them from shame. But a healthy dose of shame plays a crucial role in empathy, in leading toward regret for one's actions and attitudes, and in change.

The Bible defines Christian leadership by character, humility, service, and love. Good leadership starts with repentance, humility, and love, and a desire to listen and learn. Want to live a life that matters? Want to be a leader who serves Jesus and his church and world well? Live with integrity and humility. Value people and relationships. Love God and be a servant. Be conformed to Christ.

The church needs whistle-blowers who speak to power and challenge abusive and narcissistic leaders. But the toxic cultures that support them in churches and other Christian organisations must be confronted too.

Toxic Cultures Need To Be Confronted

Churches and Christian organisations are rife with narcissistic, controlling leaders. But these leaders don't exist in a vacuum. They are often nurtured, protected, and enabled by groups of people.

What does the Christian faith do to breed so many unaccountable, domineering, narcissistic leaders? Is it the power we give them? Is it the fact that they think they are representing God? Is it that they don't get challenged on the way up because we avoid conflict? Is it because we don't have enough models of servant leadership? Is it because we over-emphasise cognitive ability versus empathy? Is it because we don't take supervision seriously enough and fail to implement checks and balances? Is it because we put our leaders on a pedestal and don't take Jesus's words on servanthood seriously enough?

But to be fair, narcissistic leaders are often charming and persuasive. They have a way of drawing people and whole systems in and then shaping them into a haven for their disorder, egos, and control.

Narcissistic leaders create harmful churches and organisational cultures, and are made by them. The leaders usually exist within toxic (or compromised and co-dependent) groups and are inseparable from them. You can't deal with the wounding leader without dealing with the damaging church or organisational culture that protects and enables them.

How do you know if your group, church, or organisation is toxic (or is becoming toxic)? In these organisations, service and love are being replaced by power and control. Dissenters are silenced or removed. Uncritical loyalty is demanded. Some people prop up the narcissistic leader and support or enable their behaviour. Others put their head down and try to be invisible or not rock the boat, to survive. Avenues for addressing the problems are closed down, or it becomes clear that the consequences for speaking up will be severe. Intimidation is tolerated. Emotional abuse is common (e.g., minimising and denying problems, gaslighting and blaming victims, and accusing or assassinating the character of whistle-blowers). Those who speak up are isolated or removed. Coercion and threats are used to control and silence people (either subtly or overtly).

When the behaviour of a narcissistic leader or a toxic culture is challenged, the leader's peers (inside and outside the organisation) will often rally around the leader. These peers will then ignore or minimise the complaints, trying to sweep the issues under the carpet rather than address them. The whole system becomes toxic.

In his Eternity article on whistle-blowers, Michael Jensen rightly introduces the biblical metaphor of family as a corrective to more damaging and corrosive images. But it's also worth noting that family systems theories tell us a lot about how family abuse operates and how family systems can support abuse.

We often focus on an individual abuser — someone who takes advantage of their spiritual, positional, or relational power. But, there is almost always a complex system supporting them (theological, structural, interpersonal, and other). Complicity runs deep.

I'm all for confronting individual leaders when needed. But the more complicated, more complex, and dangerous, and possibly more necessary task is to engage the abusive theologies, systems, and structures that enable and even cultivate such leaders.

The loyalty we must challenge isn't just loyalty to a person; it's unwavering loyalty to a particular theology, institution, or system. Otherwise, you may end up just scapegoating the problem and avoiding the real work of collective conviction, lament, repentance, and change.

The prophet Nathan indeed confronted King David on his abuse of power. A single prophet did challenge a particular king. May God give us more Nathans.

But most of the time, the prophets and the apostles confronted collective sin. Individual repentance is essential. But very often, a whole group, church, leadership team, Board, or organisation needs to lament, repent, and change. Toxic, sinful, harmful groups and their cultures need to be challenged by whistle-blowers and by the gospel, not just individual narcissistic leaders.

Growing Healthy Leaders and Church Cultures

Recent (and ancient) high-profile leadership failings show us that leadership idols and dysfunctions are severely damaging the church and its witness. These include narcissism and pride, and the desire for (and pursuit of) status, brand, power, control, popularity, and success.

It's time for our servant-ministers to adopt a different posture and language among us and within the world – one patterned after Jesus Christ. And it's time for our churches and Christian organisations to refuse to accept anything less than accountability, humility, service, and love as the defining features of our leaders and our collective life together. Our loyalty is firstly and primarily to Jesus Christ and no one else.

Our leaders, churches, colleges, and Christian organisations must nurture a way of life (discipleship) shaped around at least these things:

- Love (including loving service).
- Kindness (being a person and community of empathy, gentleness, patience, and compassion).
- Humility (relinquishing brand, power, ego, status, and control).
- Integrity (in every aspect of life).

- Prayer (as the heart of Christian community, service, and ministry).
- Collaboration (giving yourself genuinely to the Christian community, and to cultivating unity in diversity, and unity in dissension).
- Faith (formed in trust and dependency).
- Openness (to constructive and critical feedback).
- Truth-telling (protecting and listening to whistle-blowers, and amplifying the prophetic voices and the voices of "the least of these brothers and sisters").
- Grace (honouring and esteeming others, and being gracious and forgiving).
- Discipleship (as our primary vocation and call).
- Vulnerability (weakness, transparency, vulnerability, and honesty).
- Hope (putting your legacy and efforts into a different, Christ-centred frame).

What I'm describing here is the kind of leadership and community that honours Jesus and the gospel. Will we rise to the challenge? Will we follow our crucified, self-giving, servant Lord?

Appendix: A Book Recommendation

"When Narcissism Comes to Church" by Chuck DeGroat

This is the best book I've read on narcissism in Christianity, especially among Christian leaders.

DeGroat quotes Lasch when he writes that narcissism is "longing to be freed from longing" (i.e., longing to be free of shame, failings, and humanity through visions, strivings, and masks of grandiosity. "Human limitation, fragility, and weakness hurt too much," so narcissists find ways to hide behind a mask). The narcissistic mask is grandiose, attention-seeking, entitled, and unempathetic, covering deep wells of shame, a sense of vulnerability, and a fear of being exposed as inadequate or "human." Narcissism and narcissistic systems need hiddenness and secrecy to survive, fearing that their shame and failings will be brought out into the light and avoiding the truth of weakness and vulnerability.

Christianity offers profound opportunities for people to avoid their deep inner shame, longing, and humanity through platform, performance, stage, power, branding, recognition, followers, and acclaim. "Ministry is a magnet for a narcissistic personality—who else would want to speak on behalf of God every week? While the vast majority of people struggle with public speaking . . . pastors do it regularly [and] with 'divine authority'" (page 19).

DeGroat offers so much in this work, including how enneagram personality types help us understand the nine faces and types of narcissism, how to confront and heal from narcissistic leaders and church systems, how to understand the inner life of a narcissist, and how to heal ourselves and the church from narcissistic abuse. At times, I felt his correlation between narcissistic and enneagram types was a stretch, but it was a creative and insightful framework nonetheless. I value the way DeGroat shows how narcissism is our collective problem (our church cultures and systems encourage and support narcissism, including the way we choose church planters, innovators, and leaders) and how we all need to examine our role in dealing with our inner narcissistic tendencies, especially in the age of social media.

Some of our tests for "apostolic, pioneering, innovative leaders" seem designed to reward and amplify narcissism rather than the humble, servant way of Jesus Christ. DeGroat also speaks of the characteristics of the "fauxnerable Christian leader" who uses carefully curated "vulnerability" to cover their narcissism and put the spotlight on themselves.

DeGroat believes that transformation and change for the narcissist (and narcissistic church systems) are possible, but it's a slow, painful, vulnerable, honest, and courageous process. Like so many others, I've been hurt by narcissistic Christian leaders who could not see themselves or understand the impact of their behaviours—and I've felt let down by governance groups that refused to confront narcissistic abuse. As someone who has struggled for a few years to confront my selfish tendencies and the impact it has on others (I'm not a narcissist according to clinical definitions, but, like many others, struggle against the pull toward narcissistic or selfish tendencies), I found deGroat's insights into how to heal from our inner narcissism helpful and his compassion sincere.

This is a book every Christian ministry team, board, and eldership should read as we seek to deal with the widespread narcissism among Christian leaders and church systems today.

PART III — CROSS AND COMPASSION: CRUCIFORM LOVE FOR A WOUNDED WORLD

Part III unfolds a vision of cruciform love, Christ's self-giving way that confronts hatred, heals wounds, dismantles injustice, and summons the church into courageous solidarity with all who suffer.

8. A Cruciform Witness Against Antisemitism: A Christian Call to Love, Justice, and Truth

Christians throughout the centuries have used the word "cruciform" (literally "cross-shaped") to describe a life patterned after Jesus's self-giving love.[33]

A cruciform faith is one shaped by the self-giving love of Jesus revealed on the cross. It embodies a way of being in the world characterized by humility rather than dominance, sacrifice rather than self-promotion, mercy rather than vengeance, and reconciliation rather than retaliation. To live cruciformly is to allow the pattern of Christ's cross (suffering love, poured-out compassion, enemy-embracing forgiveness, and trust in God) to form our character, guide our actions, and reshape how we see others and ourselves.

"A cruciform life is patterned after the self-giving love of Christ's cross."

A Cruciform Witness Against Antisemitism

There are wounds so ancient and so deep that they seem woven into the soil of history. Antisemitism is one of these wounds. It's older than the church, older than the modern West, older even than the languages we use to name it. It's as ancient as Pharaoh's fear, as persistent as Babylon's exile, as violent as Rome's occupation. It's changed shape across millennia (religious, racial, political, conspiratorial). Still, its intent has

---

33 Philippians 2:5–11; Mark 8:34.

remained the same: to diminish, distort, and destroy the dignity of Jewish people made in the image of God.

For followers of Jesus, opposing antisemitism isn't optional. It's a matter of discipleship. To follow the crucified and risen Lord is to stand with every people who have endured contempt, violence, and exile. But with the Jewish people, the Christian responsibility is even more intimate. The One we confess as Lord was born into Jewish flesh, prayed Jewish prayers, kept Jewish feasts, lived as a Jewish rabbi, and still bears in his resurrected body the Jewish wounds he received at the hands of empire. There is no Christian identity without Israel; no gospel without the promises made to Abraham; no salvation history without the faithfulness of a people who carried the covenant through fire.

And yet, across history, Christians have often turned the cross against the very people of Jesus. We've forgotten our own story. We've forgotten that the Messiah we worship came not to erase Israel but to fulfill God's covenantal love for Israel and, through Israel, to bless every nation on earth. When Christians forget this, antisemitism flourishes. When we remember, something healing and holy becomes possible.

This is a call to remember.

This is a call to repent.

This is a call to take up a cruciform posture (a posture shaped entirely by Jesus's self-giving love) and confront antisemitism with clarity, courage, and compassion.

This is a call to stand with the Jewish people in a wounded world, not as an act of political partisanship, but as an act of discipleship to the crucified and risen Christ.

"A cruciform life refuses to let fear become a theology or prejudice become a liturgy."

Naming the Wound: What Antisemitism Is

Antisemitism is hostility, hatred, discrimination, or violence directed toward Jewish people as Jews.[34] It takes many forms: blaming Jewish communities for social or economic problems, denying or distorting Jewish identity and history, spreading conspiracies about supposed Jewish power, desecrating synagogues, cemeteries, and sacred texts, denying or minimizing the Holocaust, targeting Jewish individuals or institutions with harassment or violence, and holding Jewish people collectively responsible for the actions of any government.

Antisemitism isn't merely an opinion or a political stance. It's a sin against the God who created every Jewish person in the divine image. It's a rejection of Jesus's own humanity. It's a wound in the Body of Christ.

And crucially:

Antisemitism isn't the same as critiquing the actions of the State of Israel.[35]

Nations (any nation) are accountable to moral scrutiny. Policies can be unjust. Governments can oppress. Leaders can sin. Christians committed to justice must be able to lament the suffering of Palestinians, name wrongdoing by the Israeli government, and advocate for the dignity and rights of all people without falling into antisemitic tropes or dehumanization.

The problem arises when criticism becomes demonization, when legitimate critique collapses into conspiratorial blame, when protest is mixed with hatred of Jews as a people, or when the language of "they" and "them" conjures the old ghosts of racialized suspicion.

"Scrutinizing the actions of any government is responsible citizenship; demonizing an entire people is sin."

The Jerusalem Declaration on Antisemitism is a welcome gift for those who long for moral clarity in a world where grief, politics, and

---

[34] International Holocaust Remembrance Alliance, "Working Definition of Antisemitism."

[35] Jewish Community Relations Council, "Criticism of Israel vs. Antisemitism."

history often collide.[36] It gathers the wisdom of hundreds of scholars who've spent their lives tracing the wounds and resilience of Jewish communities, and it offers a thoughtful alternative to frameworks that sometimes blur the lines between prejudice and legitimate political critique. By clearly marking the boundary between antisemitism and robust debate about Israel/Palestine, it creates space for truth-telling without fear, and solidarity without silence. It insists that opposing a political ideology, imagining different constitutional futures, supporting boycotts, or delivering a sharp critique of state power aren't, in themselves, antisemitic. At the same time, it draws a firm line where old hatreds re-emerge: when criticism turns Jews into a monolith, trades in ancient tropes, or smuggles contempt for a people under the cover of political anger. In doing so, the Declaration helps communities, institutions, and leaders pursue justice with cleaner hands and clearer conscience, honouring Jewish dignity while allowing open, honest engagement with the hard questions of our time.

> *"Antisemitism is discrimination, prejudice, hostility or violence against Jews as Jews (or Jewish institutions as Jewish)." – The Jerusalem Declaration on Antisemitism, 2021*

We must learn to walk with discernment: defending Jewish dignity without excusing injustice and defending Palestinian dignity without feeding the ancient hatreds that have murdered generations.

This is possible, but only with a cruciform imagination shaped by Jesus.

A Brief Christian History of Antisemitism: Confession before Action

Before Christians can speak prophetically against antisemitism, we must speak truthfully about our own history. This history isn't peripheral; it's central to why the church must now stand with clarity and humility.

---

[36] The Jerusalem Declaration on Antisemitism.

Christian antisemitism has taken many forms across the centuries: patristic writings that demonized Jews; medieval laws that segregated and impoverished Jewish communities; forced conversions and expulsions throughout Europe; crusaders who massacred entire Jewish towns; passion plays that portrayed Jewish people as Christ-killers; the silence or complicity of churches during pogroms; the theological soil that nourished European racial antisemitism; the failure of many Christians to resist the horrors of the Holocaust; and the postwar rise of Christian nationalism that continued to marginalize Jewish neighbors.[37]

This isn't ancient history. It lives beneath the surface of Christian memory. It shapes attitudes, sermons, political rhetoric, and imagination. Our task isn't to wallow in guilt but to practice confession. Confession restores truth. Confession breaks denial. Confession opens the door to healing.

A cruciform church is a confessing church.

A church that refuses confession turns the cross into an empty symbol instead of a living power.

Cruciform Vision: What Jesus Teaches Us about Antisemitism

The antidote to antisemitism isn't first political; it's theological. It begins with Jesus.

(a) Jesus Was Jewish, Is Jewish, and Remains Jewish

This truth alone destabilizes antisemitism at its root.[38] The incarnation isn't accidental. Jesus enters history in a particular people with a specific story.

To reject or demean the Jewish people is to deny the flesh that God chose to bear.

To follow Jesus is to honor his people.

---

[37] Nirenberg, *Anti-Judaism: The Western Tradition.*
[38] Luke 2; John 4; Romans 9–11.

(b) Jesus Reveals God's Covenant Fidelity to Israel

Jesus doesn't replace Israel; he fulfills God's promises to Israel. The New Testament is unintelligible apart from the story of Israel's covenant, law, prophets, temple, exile, return, and longing for redemption.

God's faithfulness to Israel isn't revoked. The church doesn't cancel Israel; it's grafted into Israel's story.

Christians who grasp this can never participate in antisemitism.

(c) Jesus Confronts the Powers that Devour People

Antisemitism isn't just hatred; it's a principality, a spiritual power that feeds on fear, projection, and violence. Jesus confronts such powers, not by mirroring their violence, but by exposing and disarming them at the cross.

The cross is God's definitive rejection of scapegoating.

A cruciform people can't scapegoat Jewish communities (or any communities) for the world's problems.

(d) Jesus Teaches Us to Love Our Neighbors and Our Enemies

This includes Jewish neighbors and Palestinian neighbors. It includes Israeli families living in fear and Palestinian families living under violence or occupation.

The command to love can't be selectively applied.

"The gospel never gives Christians permission to hate; it commands us to love even where history groans."

Love isn't agreement. Love isn't silence. Love isn't sentimentality. Love seeks justice for all, dignity for all, safety for all.

(e) Jesus Names and Heals Our Implicit Bias

Whenever we dehumanize, stereotype, or generalize about any people group, Jesus places a mirror before us. The Spirit reveals the prejudice we've inherited, absorbed, or tolerated. True discipleship requires letting this mirror change us.

"The cross teaches us that hatred of any people isn't merely wrong, it's a betrayal of the One who stretched out arms of reconciliation for the whole world."

Distinguishing Critique from Contempt: How to Speak with Moral Clarity

Christians must be able to critique any nation's actions (including Israel's) without falling into antisemitism. This requires moral discernment and spiritual maturity.

Legitimate critique includes opposing unjust policies, grieving the deaths of civilians, advocating for human rights, resisting the pull of nationalism and militarism, and calling for peace, equality, and dignity for all.

Antisemitic patterns include blaming "the Jews" as a collective, invoking conspiracies of secret control, denying Jewish indigeneity in the land, comparing Jewish self-determination to totalitarian evil, demonizing Jews as Christ-killers, using Nazi imagery irresponsibly, and ignoring the history and trauma carried by Jewish communities.

Christians must hold two truths at once:

Israel's government isn't identical with the Jewish people.

The suffering of Palestinians doesn't justify hatred of Jews.

To walk this line requires cruciform humility, not ideological certainty.

A Theology of the Cross Against Antisemitism

The cross is the center of Christian imagination. It reveals how God confronts evil and how disciples are called to respond to injustice.

Here are the cruciform principles that speak directly to antisemitism:

(a) The Cross Exposes Scapegoating

Jesus was executed by an imperial government using the logic of scapegoating: "It's better that one man die for the people." This logic fuels antisemitism. The cross unmasks it as a lie.

Any ideology that makes the Jewish people a scapegoat stands condemned by the cross.

(b) The Cross Reveals that God Stands with the Persecuted

Jesus's death aligns God with victims of violence and prejudice. Jewish communities, who endured centuries of persecution from Christian societies, are therefore not on the "outside" of God's concern: they are near the heart of it.

(c) The Cross Teaches Nonviolence, Not Revenge

Antisemitism is often rooted in grievance, real or imagined. The cross reveals that vengeance destroys the one who wields it. The cross calls us to resist evil without mirroring its methods.

(d) The Cross Forms a People of Compassion

A cross-shaped community is tenderhearted, not hard-hearted. It listens to trauma. It honors memory. It refuses to weaponize pain.

The cruciform church protects the vulnerable: Jewish and Palestinian, Israeli and Arab.

(e) The Cross Requires Truthfulness

Antisemitism thrives in conspiracy and lies. The crucified God calls the church to ruthless honesty. Truth is cruciform: humble, self-emptying, and courageous.

A Scriptural Vision for Christian Solidarity with the Jewish People

The Bible gives Christians a framework for rejecting antisemitism and standing with the Jewish people.

(a) Genesis: Every human bears the image of God

Dehumanization violates the first truth of Scripture.

(b) God's Covenant with Abraham

Christians are grafted into Israel's covenant, not the other way around. We owe gratitude, not contempt.

(c) The Prophets: Justice, Not Prejudice

The prophets confront injustice in Israel because of love for Israel. Christian critique must follow that pattern: rooted in love, never in disdain.

(d) The Gospels: Jesus within Judaism

Jesus's mission is unintelligible apart from his Jewish identity. Every Christian prayer invokes a Jewish Messiah.

(e) Romans 9–11: The irrevocable calling

Paul's vision is unequivocal: God's covenant with Israel is unbroken, and the church must never boast over the branches.

(f) Revelation: A New Jerusalem

The final hope of the Bible is a redeemed humanity gathered around the God of Israel.

If Christians truly believed these texts, antisemitism could not survive among us.

What Christian Spirituality Offers: Practices for Purifying the Heart

Rejecting antisemitism isn't only intellectual; it requires spiritual formation.

(a) The Practice of Confession

We name prejudice in ourselves and in our communities. We renounce inherited sin. We reject the "little jokes," the stereotypes, the casual cynicism.

Confession disarms the hostility lodged in the heart.

(b) Contemplation and the Purification of Perception

Contemplative prayer quiets reactivity. It allows the Spirit to reshape our gaze so we see Jewish neighbors not through the lens of politics or history, but through the eyes of Christ.

(c) Lectio Divina with the Hebrew Scriptures

Reading the Hebrew Scriptures slowly and prayerfully reconnects Christians to the spiritual ancestry we share.

(d) Fasting from Contempt

Christians can fast not only from food but from the habits of speech that perpetuate hatred. A fast from contempt may be one of the most needed spiritual disciplines of our age.

(e) Intercessory Prayer for Jewish Neighbors and Communities

Prayer forms affection. Prayer builds bridges where ideology builds walls.

How Christians Can Practically Resist Antisemitism Today

A cruciform approach includes explicit, concrete action.

(1) Challenge antisemitic tropes in conversation, churches, and online spaces.

Don't remain silent. Silence protects hatred.

(2) Build relationships with local Jewish communities.

Attend events when invited. Visit synagogues. Listen. Learn. Offer friendship with no agenda.

(3) Preach and teach about Israel's role in salvation history.

This roots Christian identity in gratitude, not supersessionism.

(4) Advocate for the safety of Jewish communities.

Support security measures, oppose harassment, and publicly condemn threats.

(5) Distinguish clearly between anti-Zionism and antisemitism.

Draw boundaries. Teach nuance. Form disciples who can lament Palestinian suffering without vilifying Jews.

(6) Support peacebuilding efforts in Israel–Palestine.

A cruciform posture longs for safety, dignity, and flourishing for both peoples.

(7) Use Scripture responsibly.

Reject weaponized interpretations. Refuse to frame Jews as spiritually blind or cursed: interpretations with deadly consequences.

> *"Wherever contempt rises, the church is called to kneel: to embody the humility of Christ that breaks cycles of suspicion and scorn."*

The Witness of a Cruciform Church

When the church stands against antisemitism, it bears witness to Jesus by embodying his love in the world.

A cruciform church refuses to be captured by political echo chambers, resists narratives of vengeance, defends the dignity of every human, and seeks justice with tenderness. It remembers the wounds of history and dares to face the truth about its own failures. It loves its Jewish neighbors with concrete fidelity, not abstraction, and labors for peace in a world shaped by violence.

This isn't a political stance but a Christ-shaped one.

The church doesn't exist to mirror the world's divisions; it exists to reveal God's reconciling love.

When Christians stand with Jewish communities, we aren't choosing one side of a worldly conflict.

"The crucified Messiah invites us into a way of being where no one is made an enemy and every neighbor becomes a sacred trust."

We are choosing the side of the crucified God, who binds up the brokenhearted and calls every people beloved.

A Prayer for Christlike Solidarity

O Christ, the wounded healer,
> born into the house of Israel,
> faithful Son of Abraham,
> teacher of mercy, bearer of truth,
> bridge between heaven and earth,
> teach us to walk your cruciform way.

Deliver us from the blindness
> that turns neighbors into threats.

Cleanse our hearts of prejudice,
> resentment, and inherited contempt.

Let the sins of our ancestors
> be confessed, not repeated.

Give us courage to confront hatred,
> wisdom to discern truth from ideology,
> and tenderness to stand with all who suffer.

Let our love be wider than our fear,
> our justice deeper than our outrage,
> our speech gentler than the world's noise.

And gather your peoples together,
> Jew and Gentile, Israeli and Palestinian,
> enemy and friend,
> beneath the shelter of your peace.

For you are our reconciliation,
> our hope,
> our center,

our Lord.

Amen.

9. A Cruciform Witness Against Anti-Palestinianism: Learning to See, Lament, and Love in the Way of Christ

There are wounds that span generations. Wounds carried not merely in flesh but in memory, in longing, in the very landscape of a people's story. For Palestinians (Christian and Muslim alike) these wounds have become a defining mark of existence: dispossession, displacement, erasure, occupation, dehumanization, restriction, suspicion, and the daily struggle to live with dignity in a land that holds both their history and their hope.

To speak of this isn't to enter a political argument; it's to name a human reality. And naming reality is the beginning of every Christian act of truthfulness.

Yet in much of the Christian world, Palestinian suffering has been minimized, spiritualized, or dismissed altogether. Their longing for safety, dignity, freedom, and belonging is too often framed as a threat, their grief as propaganda, their identity as questionable, their narrative as suspect. This pattern (where an entire people's humanity is questioned or erased) is what we call anti-Palestinianism.

What Is Anti-Palestinianism?

Anti-Palestinianism is hostility, erasure, dehumanization, or prejudice directed toward Palestinians *as Palestinians*. It includes denying the existence of the Palestinian people; dismissing their historical presence in the land; treating their suffering as fabricated; portraying them collectively as violent, irrational, or untrustworthy; or refusing to acknowledge their equal dignity and right to live in freedom, safety, and flourishing.[39]

Anti-Palestinianism manifests whenever a people's story is silenced, their grief is ignored, or their longing for justice is treated as illegitimate. At its heart is a refusal to see Palestinians as fully human: neighbors, image-bearers, and fellow children of God.

This isn't a political category. It's a moral one.

It's the sin of refusing to see the face of Christ in the Palestinian other.

The Call to See: Recovering a Cruciform Vision of the Human

Christians are summoned to see the world through the cross: to view every person, every people, every suffering face through the self-giving love of the Crucified One. A cruciform vision refuses the narratives of power that dominate the world; it resists every ideology that redraws human beings into categories of "danger," "problem," or "enemy."

A cruciform church looks first at Christ on the cross and hears him say, "Whatever you do to the least of these, you do to me."

---

[39] Zogby, *Palestinians.*

To see with a cruciform imagination is to let the cross recalibrate the way we look at wounded places and weary peoples. It's to let divine self-giving love reshape our instincts, loosen our defensiveness, and open our hearts to the ones whose pain our culture finds easiest to ignore.[40] The cross refuses selective compassion. It calls us to attend to every cry, especially the cries that get dismissed, politicized, or buried beneath the noise of competing narratives. So, when we speak of seeing cruciformly, we're speaking of a way of beholding the world that mirrors the One who carried sorrow without flinching and held humanity's ache without preference or partiality.

Seeing cruciformly means acknowledging that Palestinian suffering is real, even when that reality disrupts the stories we've grown comfortable rehearsing. It means refusing the temptation to sanitize, relativize, or explain away the trauma of communities who've lived under layers of displacement, dispossession, and daily precarity. There's nothing righteous about averting our eyes from a neighbor's wounds simply because their anguish unsettles our politics. Cruciform vision won't allow it.

Seeing cruciformly also means naming Palestinian grief as valid, even when some would prefer it remain unspoken. Grief that's silenced doesn't disappear; it hardens, festers, and isolates. A cross-shaped faith listens to lament with humility, honoring the tears of those who carry generational sorrow, fractured families, and dreams deferred. Such listening isn't a threat to anyone's security or dignity; it's a witness to truth.

To look through the lens of the cross is to affirm Palestinian dignity as inherent: not bestowed by any state or system, not earned by performance or politics, but held within every person as a gift of the One who breathes life into dust. This dignity persists even when it's denied, ignored, or violated. Cruciform witness insists on seeing what public life sometimes refuses to see.

---

[40] Gutiérrez, *A Theology of Liberation.*

And seeing cruciformly means confessing that Palestinian humanity is non-negotiable, even when public discourse treats it as expendable. Whenever a people's humanity becomes conditional, we've strayed far from the One who healed enemies and lifted the lowly. A cross-shaped vision draws us back, teaching us to resist dehumanization in all its forms.

To see cruciformly, then, is to let love take the lead. It's to let compassion grow deeper than fear, truth stronger than propaganda, and solidarity more enduring than convenience. It's to stand where the Crucified One stands (in the hard places, with the hurting ones) until our vision aligns with the holy, steady gaze of grace.

Anti-Palestinianism survives wherever Christians fail to see.

"To refuse to see a people's suffering is to refuse the face of Christ."

This vision isn't sentimental. It's the costly clarity of love. It asks the church to allow the wounds of others to pierce our indifference, to enter our prayers, to shape our moral imagination. It calls us to look at the cross and then look again at every crucified people in our world, including Palestinians.

The Sin of Erasure: When a People's Story Is Silenced

Anti-Palestinianism thrives in silence.

It appears when Palestinian identity is dismissed as invented, when their connection to the land is denied, when their stories are filtered through suspicion, when their cultural, religious, and historical presence is erased from memory and map.

It appears when Palestinian Christians are treated as theological footnotes in a land where their spiritual ancestors first confessed Jesus as Lord.

It appears when the world describes the land as empty, despite the fact that families have lived, loved, planted, worshiped, and buried generations there.

Erasure isn't merely historical. It's spiritual. It's the refusal to honor the God who plants every people in their land and breathes into every community a story worth telling.

"Erasing a people's story is a form of violence; remembering them is an act of Christian fidelity."

A cruciform people resist erasure because the gospel calls us to remember:

remember those experiencing poverty and hunger,

remember those experiencing occupation and oppression,

remember those experiencing abuse and dispossession,

remember those experiencing silencing and violence,

remember the stories that powerful empires would rather hide and bury.[41]

Critique, Conscience, and the Difference Between Justice and Antisemitism

Christian fidelity demands the courage to name injustice wherever it appears, even (and especially) when that truth is uncomfortable. To critique a government's actions isn't to condemn a people, a culture, or a faith tradition. It's simply to practice moral clarity. This distinction has been affirmed not only by theologians and ethicists across centuries but also by Jewish scholars themselves, most clearly in the Jerusalem Declaration on Antisemitism (2021). The Declaration insists that holding a state accountable for its policies isn't antisemitism, and that "criticizing or opposing Zionism as a form of nationalism" or "evidence-based criticism of Israel's laws, policies, and actions" *doesn't* constitute hatred toward Jewish people.[42] The line between critique and prejudice is real, but it's neither thin nor fragile.

---

[41] See the Kairos Document and the Kairos II Document.

[42] See *The Jerusalem Declaration on Antisemitism* and also Jewish Community Relations Council, "Criticism of Israel vs. Antisemitism."

Israel is a state with political power, military capacity, and responsibility under international law. Naming the harm endured by Palestinians (including displacement, occupation, systemic inequality, and restrictions on movement) isn't an attack on Jewish identity; it's a refusal to let suffering go unacknowledged. When Christians speak truthfully about these realities, they're not entering a partisan debate but responding to a biblical imperative: to defend the oppressed, to honor every person's dignity, and to resist systems that diminish life.

The Jerusalem Declaration reminds us that antisemitism is a hatred directed at *Jews as Jews*. Justice-oriented critique is directed at political actions, structures, and systems. Confusing the two only protects the powerful and obscures the plight of the powerless.

In fact, refusing to lament Palestinian suffering for fear of being misunderstood can itself become a form of moral evasion. Genuine solidarity with Jewish communities must walk hand-in-hand with genuine solidarity with Palestinians. One love doesn't cancel the other.

To tell the truth about injustice isn't to abandon compassion for Jewish neighbors; it's to honor the prophetic legacy they've given the world: a legacy that calls us all to seek justice, love mercy, and refuse every form of dehumanization.

Distinguishing Prophetic Critique from Anti-Palestinianism

Christians must learn the discipline of moral clarity.

A cruciform life doesn't ask us to suspend moral judgment; it invites us to deepen it. Scripture calls us to name injustice, confront wrongdoing, and discern between paths that lead to life and paths that lead to harm. It's never unfaithful to critique destructive actions taken by any person, community, or authority. Moral clarity is part of discipleship. Truth-telling is part of love. And a commitment to justice requires that we hold all people, including ourselves, accountable for the ways we wound others.

But critique becomes something else (something corrosive and contrary to the way of the cross) when it slips into anti-Palestinianism. This happens when the actions of a few are projected onto an entire people, as though a whole community can be reduced to the worst choices of some. Such sweeping judgments flatten complexity, erase nuance, and create distance where compassion should dwell.

It becomes anti-Palestinian when Palestinians are cast as inherently violent or somehow less deserving of the rights every human should enjoy. When rhetoric frames a people as fundamentally suspect, morally deficient, or perpetually threatening, it's no longer the work of truth-seeking; it's the work of dehumanization. A cross-shaped imagination refuses these narratives because they contradict the very heart of the Gospel: a Gospel that insists every life bears divine breath.

Anti-Palestinianism shows itself when Palestinian claims to safety, freedom, and dignity are dismissed or downplayed. When legitimate longing for justice is recast as instability or danger, or when political calculations mute calls for fundamental human rights, we betray the biblical call to stand with the oppressed and to hear the cry of those pushed to the margins.

It's anti-Palestinian when Palestinian voices are excluded from the conversations that determine their futures. Silencing a people (whether through fear, bureaucracy, or paternalistic narratives) undermines any honest pursuit of peace. A cruciform community listens first, especially to those whose agency has been ignored or constrained.

And it becomes anti-Palestinian when Palestinian grief is treated as exaggerated, manipulative, or suspect. Grief is sacred. Tears reveal truth. When a people's sorrow is interrogated instead of honored, we drift far from the One who gathers every lament with tenderness.

To walk the way of the cross is to cultivate a moral discernment shaped by compassion, not caricature; by justice, not fear. It's to critique what harms, while refusing to diminish the humanity of those who suffer. In a time of hardened narratives and quick condemnation, cruciform love calls us back to honesty, humility, and the fierce defense of every person's dignity.

> *"Critique is moral; dehumanization is sin. Christians must know the difference."*

Christians can and should speak with moral clarity about violence wherever it appears. But a cruciform witness insists that judgment never collapses into hatred, suspicion, or collective blame. Justice without love becomes vengeance; love without justice becomes sentimentality. The way of Christ holds both together.

The Witness of Palestinian Christians

One of the great tragedies of Christian discourse is how seldom Palestinian Christians are heard within the global church. Yet their witness is essential: both spiritually and morally.

For centuries, Palestinian Christians have carried the gospel in the very land where it was first preached.[43] They have endured injustice, displacement, discrimination, and loss, yet have preserved a vibrant theology of hope. Their voices echo the biblical prophets: calling the church to truthfulness, justice, reconciliation, and nonviolent resistance grounded in the love of Christ.

They remind us that the Christian story in the land isn't foreign, imported, or recent. It's ancient, rooted, and alive.

Their cries aren't abstract. They're concrete:

We long to live in dignity.
We long for freedom.
We long for safety.
We long for peace for all our neighbors.

---

[43] Raheb, *Faith in the Face of Empire.*

We long to raise our children without fear.

These longings are profoundly Christian longings.

To ignore Palestinian Christians is to silence part of the body of Christ.

A Cruciform Approach: What the Way of Jesus Requires

A cruciform approach is a way of seeing and living shaped by the cross.

A cruciform church doesn't measure its faithfulness by its influence, its reputation, or its proximity to the powerful. It measures faithfulness by its willingness to stand where the Crucified One stands: near the wounded, the weary, and the forgotten. To live this way is costly. It requires a community shaped not by fear or ideology, but by the love that poured itself out for the healing of the world.

Such a church centers the suffering of others rather than the comfort of the privileged. It listens before it speaks, attends before it defends, and draws near to those most easily overlooked. It recognizes that the Gospel always moves toward the broken places, and so it follows that movement with trembling courage.

A cruciform church breaks cycles of vengeance by absorbing pain with mercy. It refuses to mirror the world's violence back into the world. It bears witness to the truth that retaliation never brings restoration. That mercy (costly, patient, persistent mercy) is the only force strong enough to interrupt the spirals of harm that tear communities apart.

It refuses narratives that demand an enemy. Whenever public life is reduced to sides, camps, and foes, the cross stands as a quiet but unyielding contradiction. The cruciform community won't let fear harden into suspicion or suspicion harden into hatred. It remembers that every person, even the antagonistic or mistaken, carries a story held by divine compassion.

Such a church resists every theology that turns people into problems. It rejects doctrines that justify exclusion, diminish dignity, or baptize injustice. Instead, it seeks the kind of theological imagination that sees every person as a bearer of divine breath, every community as capable of renewal, and every conflict as a place where truth and grace can meet.

A cruciform church renounces violence as a means of healing. It trusts that peace can't be manufactured through coercion or domination. It knows that wounds don't close when inflicted by force, but when met with courage, repentance, and tenderness.

It prays for those on every side of conflict: not as a way of avoiding hard truths, but as a way of keeping its heart from calcifying. Prayer expands the soul until it can hold the grief of all.

And it advocates for justice without hatred. It names wrongs clearly, defends the oppressed boldly, and confronts systems honestly, yet always with the compassion of Christ. Its work isn't to win, but to heal.

A cruciform church embraces the world's wounded ones with open arms, trusting that love, poured out without fear, is still the path by which new creation breaks in.

"To be cruciform is to be shaped by the self-giving love of Christ on the cross: where power becomes service, justice becomes mercy, and reconciliation becomes the final word."

A cruciform witness doesn't minimize evil. It confronts it.

But it confronts evil without becoming evil.

A cruciform church refuses to baptize injustice with religious rhetoric. It refuses to sanctify inequality. It refuses to call oppression "peace."

It stands alongside every people who suffer: not with weapons, but with presence; not with slogans, but with solidarity; not with despair, but with resurrection hope.

The Christian Mandate: Love Your Palestinian Neighbor

Jesus did not give us permission to choose who counts as neighbor. Neighborliness isn't a matter of geography but of willingness.

The command is clear:

"Love your neighbor as yourself."

And even more radically:

"Love your enemies."

And even more shockingly:

"Whatever you do to the least of these, you do to me."

A Christian ethic of neighbor-love doesn't let us choose which neighbors count. It doesn't ask us to measure whose story is easier to hear or whose suffering is simpler to explain. It pulls us toward the places where compassion is contested and where human dignity is debated. It insists that love must be wide enough, brave enough, and patient enough to hold the pain of every community caught in the shadows of conflict.

Such love refuses prejudice against Palestinians. It confronts the quiet biases that shape our imagination, the inherited assumptions that narrow our compassion, and the political narratives that make some lives appear less grievable. Neighbor-love dismantles these distortions because it knows that fear never tells the truth about anyone.

Neighbor-love listens to Palestinian voices, not as an act of charity, but as an act of justice. When a people's experience is minimized or ignored, the body of Christ becomes less whole. Listening restores sight. It opens space for truth to surface, for testimony to be honored, and for healing to begin.

To honor Palestinian humanity is to affirm that no circumstance, ideology, or history can erase the God-given dignity carried in every life. It's to recognize the image of God in every Palestinian child, whose future shouldn't be determined by violence, displacement, or despair. Their laughter, their learning, their flourishing, all of it belongs to the sacred.

A Christian ethic of neighbor-love prays for freedom, safety, and dignity for all people in the land. Such prayer isn't sentimental; it's a spiritual protest against systems that diminish life. It's a refusal to accept that injustice is inevitable.

And this love steadfastly rejects narratives that demonize one people to vindicate another. The cross exposes such thinking as false, for it reveals a love that refuses to weaponize suffering or scapegoat entire communities.

To love our neighbor (every neighbor) is to stand where Christ stands: with truth, with mercy, with courage, and with a compassion big enough to heal what fear divides.

"To love Christ is to love the Palestinian neighbor; the two can't be separated."

Neighbor-love isn't partisan.

Neighbor-love is cruciform.

Neighbor-love asks:

Who is being wounded?

Whose humanity is being denied?

Whose story isn't being heard?

How can we stand alongside them in the spirit of Christ?

The Spiritual Discipline of Lament

Before Christians speak, we must learn to weep.

Lament isn't weakness. It's the refusal to let the world's pain be normalized or silenced. Lament is how Christians tell the truth: before God and before one another.[44]

---

[44] Brueggemann, *The Prophetic Imagination.*

A cruciform witness doesn't begin with arguments or positions; it begins with tears. It starts in the place where words tremble and fall quiet, where the heart can no longer pretend that suffering is abstract or distant. Lament is the first language of love in a wounded world. It refuses to rush past sorrow. It refuses to let politics dilute compassion. It lets grief soften us until we can see others as God sees them: beloved, precious, irreplaceable.

So, a cruciform witness against anti-Palestinianism begins with lament for every life lost. Every life (named or unnamed, noticed or forgotten) matters to God. To grieve these losses is to resist the lie that some deaths are less tragic or less worthy of mourning.

It laments every home destroyed, each one a universe of memories, meals, and stories. When a home falls, a world collapses with it. Lament keeps us from treating rubble as a statistic instead of a shattered sanctuary.

It laments every mother grieving. No theology is sound if it can't sit with a mother's tears. Their grief is holy ground. To honor it is to honor the heart of God.

A cruciform witness laments every child who's afraid, whose nights are filled with explosions rather than dreams. Children should learn to read and run and hope, not to hide.

It laments every young person who's known too much violence, who carries trauma too heavy for their years. Their wounds aren't collateral; they're a call to conscience.

And it laments every elder who dies still longing for peace. These are souls who've prayed across decades of disappointment, still carrying a flicker of hope for a dawn they never saw.

Lament isn't weakness. It's the courage to feel what the world refuses to feel. It's the church's first act of truth-telling. It's how cruciform witness begins: by letting the sorrow of others become our own, trusting that God meets us in those tears and leads us toward justice, mercy, and peace.

Lament keeps our hearts human.

It protects us from despair and from apathy.

It trains our spirits to hope.

"Lord, teach us to weep where you weep and hope where you hope."

The Hope That Doesn't Yield

Christian hope is neither naïve nor escapist.

Hope gazes directly at suffering: not to explain it, but to proclaim that suffering isn't the final word.

Hope believes that the God who raised Jesus from the dead will raise justice from the ashes, peace from the ruins, and new life from the rubble of history.

Hope sustains the Palestinian parent teaching their child to dream.

Hope strengthens the peacemaker refusing to hate.

Hope empowers the church to speak truth without fear and love without limit.

A cruciform church proclaims a gospel that refuses despair.

A Cruciform Prayer

O Christ,

who walks among the wounded,

teach us to walk with you in the places

where pain is real and hope is fragile.

Break our addiction to comfort

and draw us toward those who suffer.

Free us from the fear that blinds us to another's humanity.

Deliver us from the lies that divide and the hatred that destroys.

Give us the courage to name injustice

and the tenderness to seek healing.

Let our witness be shaped by your cross,

our hope anchored in your resurrection,

our love wide enough to embrace every neighbor,

including our Palestinian neighbor.

And make us instruments of your peace

until justice and mercy meet
and all your children flourish.
Amen.

10. The Centrality of Jesus Christ for Christian Discipleship and Spirituality

There's a center to all things, and it's not us.

In an age where the self is enthroned and every voice declares its own truth, Christian faith makes a startling claim: that the true center of reality, of faith, of creation itself, isn't an idea or a moral code, but a person: Jesus Christ. In him, divine love takes flesh; in him, the mystery of God is made visible; in him, the world is reconciled to its Creator.

This conviction isn't one doctrine among many; it's the beating heart of Christianity. Everything else flows from it. Every act of worship, every prayer, every movement of justice, every hope for redemption finds its beginning and end in the living Christ.

The Scriptures call him "the image of the invisible God," "the Word made flesh," "the Alpha and the Omega."[45] He isn't one revelation among others, but *the* revelation: the face of God turned toward us in mercy. To confess Christ is to say that all things hold together in him, that apart from him the cosmos falls into chaos and the human heart into despair.

This is where discipleship begins: not with programs or performance, but with a Person. It starts with falling in love with the one who first loved us.

---

[45] Colossians 1:15; John 1:14; Revelation 1:8.

The Center That Holds

At the heart of the Christian vision stands a paradox: the infinite God became finite, the eternal entered time, the Creator walked among the created. The logic of Christianity is incarnational: divine glory revealed not in domination but in vulnerability, not in distance but in nearness.

Jesus isn't merely the messenger of salvation; he is salvation. In his life, we see what it means to be human; in his death, we see the cost of love; in his resurrection, we see the dawn of a new creation.

To center faith on Christ means that everything else (church, doctrine, morality, mission) must orbit around this gravitational heart. The danger in every generation is to shift that center: to make Christianity about ethics without grace, spirituality without flesh, or activism without the cross. But when Jesus ceases to be the center, faith becomes ideology, and discipleship becomes performance.

The apostle Paul saw this clearly. To the Corinthians, who prized wisdom and power, he wrote, "I resolved to know nothing among you except Jesus Christ and him crucified."[46] To the Colossians, who were tempted by spiritual hierarchies, he declared that Christ is the one "in whom all the fullness of God was pleased to dwell."[47]

Christian faith, in all its depth and breadth, rests on this unshakable truth: that God has spoken once and for all in the Son.

"When Jesus ceases to be the center, faith becomes ideology, and discipleship becomes performance."

The Word Made Flesh

The revelation of God in Christ isn't abstract; it's embodied. Jesus doesn't simply speak the Word: he *is* the Word. His every gesture, silence, and act of compassion reveals the nature of divine love.

---

[46] 1 Corinthians 2:2.
[47] Colossians 1:19.

When he touches the leper, he declares that no one is untouchable. When he blesses the poor, he unmasks the false gods of wealth and power. When he washes the feet of his disciples, he redefines greatness as servanthood. And when he stretches out his arms on the cross, he opens the arms of God to the whole world.

"Jesus isn't merely the messenger of salvation; he is salvation."

The cross, then, isn't divine failure but divine triumph: the moment when the self-giving love of God unmasks and overcomes the powers of sin and death. Here we see the truth about God and the truth about ourselves: that real strength is found in love, that victory comes through sacrifice, and that forgiveness, not vengeance, is the deepest law of the universe.

This Christ-shaped vision defines not only theology but spirituality. To pray in his name is to enter into his compassion. To follow him is to take up the cross and love the world as he did. To worship him is to be drawn into the self-emptying life of God, where giving and receiving become one act of grace.

Discipleship as Abiding

To be a disciple isn't merely to admire Jesus: it's to abide in him. He himself said, "Abide in me as I abide in you . . . apart from me you can do nothing."[48]

Discipleship, then, isn't an achievement but a relationship. It's not primarily about moral effort but about intimacy. It's learning to dwell in Christ as branches dwell in the vine: to draw life from his presence and bear fruit that reveals his character.

This abiding is sustained by the Spirit, who glorifies Christ by forming his likeness within us. The Spirit takes what is true of Jesus and makes it true of us: his compassion becomes our compassion, his courage our courage, his humility our humility. The Spirit doesn't lead us away from Christ but deeper into him.

---

[48] John 15:4–5.

The fruit of this abiding is love: love that is patient in suffering, steadfast in justice, and gentle with the weak. In a culture addicted to outrage and self-promotion, such love is revolutionary. It exposes the idols of our age and reveals another way of being human: the way of the crucified and risen Lord.

The Cross at the Center

If Christ is the center of faith, then the cross is the center of Christ. It's the axis upon which history turns: the moment when divine love descends to the lowest depths and fills them with glory.

We must resist every temptation to domesticate the cross into a symbol of comfort or tribal victory. The cross is scandal and wisdom at once. It exposes every form of religious pride, nationalistic idolatry, and self-justifying power. It reveals the truth about the world (that injustice claims innocent lives) and the truth about God (that love extends even there and redeems).

To be a disciple of Jesus is to live under the sign of the cross. It's to let self-giving love become the pattern of our lives. This cruciform way transforms how we use power, how we treat enemies, how we handle wealth, and how we respond to suffering. It's not the way of the strong, but of the meek; not the way of control, but of surrender.

When Christians forget the cross, they lose the gospel. But when they remember it, they become a living contradiction to the world's logic of domination. The church's authority in the world doesn't come from coercion but from cruciform love: power that serves, wisdom that forgives, and truth that liberates.

The Resurrection and the New Creation

The story doesn't end in crucifixion; it bursts into resurrection. The empty tomb isn't a mere historical footnote: it's the explosion of new creation within the old.

The resurrection proclaims that death doesn't have the final word, that despair isn't destiny, and that every wound can be transfigured. In the risen Christ, humanity and divinity are united forever; creation is reclaimed, renewed, and reoriented toward its true end.

For Christian spirituality, this means that hope isn't optional; it's essential. Hope isn't optimism; it's resurrection realism: the conviction that the same power that raised Jesus from the dead is at work to renew all things.

To live in resurrection light is to practice defiant joy in the midst of darkness, to labor for justice even when the outcome is uncertain, and to see in every broken place the possibility of life again. It's to live as Easter people in a Good Friday world: refusing despair because Christ is risen, and therefore everything can change.

The Spirit Who Glorifies Christ

Jesus promised that the Spirit would come, not to replace him, but to make him present everywhere. "He'll glorify me," Jesus said, "because he'll take what is mine and declare it to you."[49]

The Spirit's work is to draw the world toward Christ, to make his love tangible in communities of faith, and to empower believers to bear witness to him in word and deed. The Spirit opens the Scriptures, illumines conscience, comforts the broken, and convicts the proud.

In a fragmented world, the Spirit forms a people whose unity isn't sameness but shared surrender to Christ's lordship. In them, the world glimpses a foretaste of the kingdom; a community of reconciliation where barriers fall and enemies become siblings.

When the Spirit glorifies Christ in us, discipleship becomes more than personal piety; it becomes participation in God's mission to renew creation. The Spirit sends us into the world not to dominate it, but to serve, to love, to heal: to make visible the reign of the crucified King.

---

[49] John 16:14–15.

Christ and the Scriptures

The Bible finds its center and coherence in Christ. He's the key that unlocks its meaning, the thread that ties its many voices into one harmony.

From Genesis to Revelation, the story unfolds toward him: the Word through whom creation was made, the promise to Abraham fulfilled, the wisdom of the prophets embodied, the law perfected in love. On the road to Emmaus, Jesus himself taught the disciples to read Scripture this way: "Beginning with Moses and all the Prophets, he interpreted to them what was said in all the Scriptures concerning himself."[50]

> *"To read the Bible apart from Christ is to risk distortion; to read it in him is to hear the heartbeat of divine love."*

To read the Bible apart from Christ is to risk distortion: to turn living Word into dead letter, grace into law, mercy into judgment. But to read it in him is to hear again the heartbeat of divine love running through every page.

This Christ-centered reading transforms the way we live. It calls us not to use Scripture as a weapon but to embody it as a witness: to let the Word become flesh again in our speech, our compassion, and our communities.

The Church Shaped by Christ

If Christ is the center of faith, he must also be the center of the church. The church exists not to preserve itself, but to proclaim and embody the reign of Christ. It's not an institution of perfection, but a community of grace, gathered around Word and Table, living from his life and for his glory.

---

[50] Luke 24:27.am the way

To be the church is to participate in the ongoing incarnation of Christ's love in the world. It means practicing forgiveness in a culture of blame, generosity in a culture of greed, truth-telling in a culture of spin, and hospitality in a culture of exclusion.

The measure of a church's faithfulness isn't its size, wealth, or influence, but its resemblance to Christ: the crucified servant, risen Lord, and friend of sinners. When the church forgets this, it becomes just another tribe among tribes. But when it remembers, it becomes what it was meant to be: a sign of the kingdom, a living parable of reconciliation, a foretaste of new creation.

The Way, the Truth, and the Life

Jesus said, "I am the way, and the truth, and the life."[51] These aren't abstract claims: they describe the shape of discipleship.

He's *the way*: we follow his path of humility, service, and sacrificial love.

He's *the truth*: not an idea to be possessed, but a person to be known and obeyed.

He's *the life*: the source of every breath, the fountain of grace that never runs dry.

To center our spirituality on Christ is to orient every part of life around this reality. Our prayer becomes a conversation with him; our ethics become an imitation of him; our mission becomes an extension of his love. Every vocation (teacher, builder, parent, professor, truck driver, nurse, politician, artist, farmer) becomes sacred when done in his name.

And when the world tempts us toward despair, Christ remains the anchor of hope. His lordship isn't tyranny but tenderness; his authority isn't domination but deliverance.

---

[51] John 14:6.

105

Christ and the Renewal of the World

The gospel of Christ isn't private. It's public, cosmic, political, and personal all at once. The reign of Jesus disrupts every empire that claims ultimate allegiance. His kingdom isn't of this world, but it's for this world: healing, reconciling, renewing.

When Christ is central, justice and mercy aren't optional add-ons to faith; they are its fruits. The Spirit who conforms us to Christ also sends us into the broken places to bear witness to his reconciling power. To live "in Christ" is to share his mission: to proclaim good news to the poor, to set captives free, to bind up the brokenhearted.

The world won't believe in Christ because we win arguments, but because we embody his love. The credibility of the gospel depends on whether the church embodies the likeness of Jesus. A Christ-centered faith must always become a Christ-shaped life: merciful, courageous, cruciform, and full of joy.

"The world wont' believe in Christ because we win arguments, but because we embody his love."

The Abiding Center

To center everything on Christ isn't a one-time decision but a lifelong conversion. Again and again, the Spirit calls us back from distraction to devotion, from ideology to intimacy, from pride to praise.

Discipleship begins in encounter and ends in communion. Spirituality begins in seeking and ends in union. Christ is the Alpha and the Omega of the journey, the companion along the way, the destination itself.

In him, our restless hearts find rest.

In him, our divided lives find wholeness.

In him, our stories (fractured, fragile, unfinished) find redemption.

When every other foundation shakes, this center still holds. For the one who said, "I am with you always," remains the same yesterday, today, and forever.[52]

A Prayer for Christ to Be the Center

O Christ, the center of all things,
> draw us out of our scattered lives into your radiant unity.

Still, the noise within us until your voice becomes clear.
Disarm our fears, heal our idols, reorder our loves.
Let your cross shape our hearts,
> your resurrection renew our hope,

> your Spirit form our words and works into instruments of peace.

Teach us to follow you with courage,
> to love with your compassion,

> to serve with your joy.

And when we forget, call us back again
> to the simple center of it all;

> your living presence,

> your unchanging grace,

> your everlasting kingdom.

Amen.

"For from him and through him and to him are all things. To him be glory forever. Amen." (Romans 11:36)

Epilogue: Christ Before Us, Christ Within Us, Christ Our Center

The call now is simple, though never small: return to Christ with an undivided heart. In an age that scatters our attention, fragments our loyalties, and pulls our desires in a thousand directions, the invitation of Jesus remains steady and unchanging. He asks not for a portion of our lives but for the whole. Not a corner of our imagination, but the center. Not polite admiration but a surrendered, radiant, courageous devotion.

To place Christ at the center isn't an intellectual exercise. It's a reordering of the soul. It's allowing Christ to reshape what we long for, what we fear, what we chase, and what we resist. It's letting the cruciform beauty of Jesus interrupt the lesser loves that so easily preoccupy us. It's trusting that the One who poured himself out in love is the only One safe enough, and strong enough, to hold our entire being.

When Christ becomes the gravitational center, everything else finds its true size. Ideologies loosen their grip. Enemies regain their humanity. Power becomes service. Identity becomes a gift. Community becomes a place of repentance, tenderness, courage, and truth. We stop trying to protect our own small kingdoms and learn to welcome the kingdom that has already drawn near.

A Christ-centered life isn't narrow; it's expansive. It leaves no room for tribalism, bitterness, or fear, because it lives from a deeper well. It doesn't deny sorrow or skip past injustice; it carries these realities into the presence of the One whose wounds hold the world together. Christ heals divisions not by erasing difference but by forming a people who refuse to give their ultimate allegiance to anything but his crucified and risen love.

This is the steady and deeply rooted transformation the church longs for. Not spectacle, but surrender. Not triumphalism, but truth. Not frantic striving, but abiding presence. When Christ is our center, holiness becomes joy, justice becomes love in public, and discipleship becomes the slow, beautiful work of becoming like him.

So as you close this book, hear the summons that threads through every chapter:

Turn your face toward Christ.

Let him reorder what you desire.

Let him purify what you trust.

Let him renew what you imagine possible.

Let him heal what has been fractured in you and around you.

Christ before you as your path.

Christ within you as your strength.

Christ beneath you as your foundation.

Christ above you as your hope.

Christ around you as your community.

Christ at the center: always, only, endlessly.

The world will keep tugging you toward distraction, fear, and fragmentation. But the Spirit keeps speaking a deeper truth: your life holds together in Christ, and only in Christ.

Return to him.

Abide in him.

Let your whole being revolve around his love.

For when Christ becomes our center, we become whole.

Bibliography

Anonymous. *The Cloud of Unknowing*. Translated by Carmen Acevedo Butcher. Boston: Shambhala, 2009.

Augustine. *On Christian Doctrine*. Translated by D. W. Robertson, Jr. Indianapolis: Bobbs-Merrill, 1958.

Barth, Karl. *Church Dogmatics IV/3.1: The Doctrine of Reconciliation*. Edited by G. W. Bromiley and T. F. Torrance. Edinburgh: T&T Clark, 1961.

Bonhoeffer, Dietrich. *Discipleship*. Translated by Barbara Green and Reinhard Krauss. Minneapolis: Fortress, 2001.

Brueggemann, Walter. *The Prophetic Imagination*. Minneapolis: Fortress, 2001.

Guigo II. *The Ladder of Monks and Twelve Meditations*. Translated by Edmund Colledge and James Walsh. Kalamazoo: Cistercian, 1979.

Gutiérrez, Gustavo. *A Theology of Liberation: History, Politics, and Salvation*. Maryknoll: Orbis, 1988.

Hawes, Jennifer Berry. *Grace Will Lead Us Home: The Charleston Church Massacre and the Hard, Inspiring Journey to Forgiveness*. New York: St. Martin's, 2019.

International Holocaust Remembrance Alliance. "Working Definition of Antisemitism." https://holocaustremembrance.com/resources/working-definition-antisemitism (2016)

Jewish Community Relations Council. "Criticism of Israel vs. Antisemitism." https://jcrc.org/blog/criticism-of-israel-vs-antisemitism/

John of the Cross, St. *Dark Night of the Soul.* Translated by E. Allison Peers. New York: Image, 1959.

John of the Cross, St. *The Collected Works of St. John of the Cross.* Translated by Kieran Kavanaugh and Otilio Rodriguez. Washington: ICS, 1991.

Julian of Norwich. *Revelations of Divine Love.* Translated by Elizabeth Spearing. London: Penguin, 1998.

Kairos Palestine. *Kairos Document: A Moment of Truth: A Word of Faith, Hope, and Love from the Heart of Palestinian Suffering.* Bethlehem: Kairos Palestine, 2009.

Kairos Palestine. *Kairos II Document: A Moment of Truth: Faith in a Time of Genocide.* Bethlehem: Kairos Palestine, 2025.

Klein, Ezra. "Spencer Cox Wants to Pull Our Politics Back From the Brink." Sep 19, 2025. The Ezra Klein Show. https://podcasts.apple.com/au/podcast/spencer-cox-wants-to-pull-our-politics-back-from-the-brink/id1548604447?i=1000727478586

Kraybill, Donald B. et al. *Amish Grace: How Forgiveness Transcended Tragedy.* San Francisco: Jossey-Bass, 2007.

Kreider, Alan. *The Patient Ferment of the Early Church: The Improbable Rise of Christianity in the Roman Empire.* Grand Rapids: Baker Academic, 2016.

Luther, Martin. *To the Christian Nobility of the German Nation* (1520). In *Three Treatises.* Translated by Charles M. Jacobs. Philadelphia: Fortress, 1970.

Mazower, Mark. *On Antisemitism: A Word in History.* London: Allen Lane, 2025.

Merton, Thomas. *New Seeds of Contemplation.* New York: New Directions, 2007.

Moltmann, Jürgen. *The Crucified God: The Cross of Christ as the Foundation and Criticism of Christian Theology.* Minneapolis: Fortress, 1993.

Nirenberg, David. *Anti-Judaism: The Western Tradition.* New York: W. W. Norton, 2013.

Nouwen, Henri J. M. *The Return of the Prodigal Son: A Story of Homecoming.* New York: Image, 1992.

Nouwen, Henri J. M. *The Wounded Healer: Ministry in Contemporary Society.* New York: Image, 1979.

Raheb, Mitri. *Faith in the Face of Empire: The Bible Through Palestinian Eyes.* Maryknoll: Orbis, 2014.

Rilke, Rainer Maria. *Letters to a Young Poet.* Translated by Stephen Mitchell. New York: Vintage International, 1984.

Rutledge, Fleming. *The Crucifixion: Understanding the Death of Jesus Christ.* Grand Rapids: Eerdmans, 2015.

The Jerusalem Declaration on Antisemitism. https://jerusalemdeclaration.org/ (2021)

Torrance, Thomas F. *The Mediation of Christ.* Colorado Springs: Helmers & Howard, 1992.

Weil, Simone. *Waiting for God.* Translated by Emma Craufurd. New York: Harper & Row, 1951.

Willard, Dallas. *The Divine Conspiracy: Rediscovering Our Hidden Life in God.* San Francisco: HarperSanFrancisco, 1998.

Williams, Rowan. *Christ the Heart of Creation.* London: Bloomsbury Continuum, 2018.

Wright, N. T. *Jesus and the Victory of God.* Minneapolis: Fortress, 1996.

Zehr, Howard. *The Little Book of Restorative Justice.* Intercourse: Good Books, 2002.

Zogby, James J. *Palestinians: The Invisible Victims: Political Zionism and the Roots of Palestinian Dispossession.* Washington: Institute for Palestine Studies, 1988.

Appendix 1: Discussion Guide

The Death of Vengeance, the Birth of Grace: Unlearning the Language of Vengeance

1. Where do you feel the pull toward retaliation, defensiveness, or grievance, and how might Christ's self-giving love invite you into a different posture?
2. In what ways has vengeance (personal, political, cultural) shaped your imagination more than forgiveness?
3. How does the cross expose the futility of "getting even," and what would it look like for you to embody cruciform mercy in genuine relationships?
4. Where have you absorbed cultural narratives that glorify dominance or retribution, and how is Jesus challenging those scripts?
5. What practices could help you become a person who disarms violence rather than mirrors it?

Let's Stop Talking about Masculinity and Start Talking about Discipleship

1. Where have cultural models of masculinity shaped your identity more than the tenderness, humility, and courage of Jesus?
2. How do the teachings and actions of Christ challenge the rigid or harmful versions of masculinity you've seen in church or society?
3. What might healing look like for men who have been wounded by shame, expectation, or performance?

4. How can communities cultivate a vision of Christlike strength, one marked by vulnerability, compassion, and integrity?

5. What would change if you (or your community) embraced a more cruciform vision of power and leadership?

Exvangelicals and the Exodus: Spiritual Lessons for Deconstructing Faith

1. What stories of spiritual hurt or disillusionment have shaped your understanding of why people leave the church?

2. How might Christ invite us to listen to exvangelicals not with defensiveness but with compassion and humility?

3. Where has the church's culture, not Christ, driven people away, and what repentance might be required?

4. How can communities create spaces of honest questioning, reconstruction, and healing for those on the margins?

5. What would it mean for your community to embody a welcoming, Christ-centered faith rather than a boundary-policing identity?

Doubt and Discipleship to Jesus: How Christian Spirituality Guides Our Way

1. When have you experienced doubt, and how did it shape, or reshape, your faith?

2. How does Jesus meet doubters in the Gospels, and what does that reveal about God's posture toward our own questions?

3. What fears make us resist acknowledging doubt, and how might Christ be inviting us into greater honesty and trust?

4. How can faith communities create a culture where asking hard questions is part of discipleship rather than a threat to it?

5. What spiritual practices help you remain open to Christ's presence even when certainty feels impossible?

How the Bible Shapes Christian Discipleship and Spirituality

1. How has the Bible functioned in your life, as a weapon, a rulebook, a story, a meeting place, or something else?
2. What does it mean to approach Scripture as a place of encounter with the living Christ rather than a tool for argument or certainty?
3. Which parts of Scripture draw you closer to Jesus, and which challenge you to rethink your assumptions?
4. How might a Christ-centered reading of Scripture reshape your views on discipleship, justice, mission, and community?
5. What rhythms of Scripture reading could help you deepen your love for Jesus rather than merely increase information?

Keeping Christ at the Center: Resisting Idolatry in an Age of Distraction

1. What "almost-Christ" idols (politics, certainty, reputation, nostalgia, leaders, purity, progress) most tempt your community?
2. How do good things become idols in churches, and where have you seen this drift in your own life or tradition?
3. What does it feel like when Christ is no longer the functional center of a community?
4. What practices of repentance, stillness, worship, or hospitality could help re-center your life on Jesus?
5. How might your community be transformed if Christ's humility, truth, and tenderness became its gravitational center?

Whistle-Blowing Glorifies Christ: Challenging Narcissistic Leaders and Toxic Cultures

1. How have you seen narcissistic or controlling leadership distort communities and overshadow Christ's presence?
2. Why is truth-telling an act of discipleship, and what fears keep us silent in the face of abuse or injustice?

3. How does the example of Christ challenge the church to confront harmful leadership with courage, truth, and compassion?
4. What safeguards (spiritual, structural, and communal) help prevent toxic cultures from forming or persisting?
5. How can your community become a place where vulnerability, humility, and accountability flourish?

A Cruciform Witness Against Antisemitism

1. How does Jesus's Jewish identity reshape the way Christians should understand antisemitism, past and present?
2. Where have harmful stereotypes or inherited interpretations shaped Christian imagination about Jewish people?
3. How does the cross, God's self-giving love, expose and confront antisemitism in the church and society?
4. What does it mean to hold together love for Jewish neighbors and concern for justice in the Middle East without collapsing into hatred?
5. What habits of confession, learning, and solidarity could help Christians resist antisemitism with clarity and compassion?

A Cruciform Witness Against Anti-Palestinianism

1. How have Palestinian stories been ignored, silenced, or stereotyped within Christian communities, and why does this matter?
2. What does the cruciform way of Jesus teach us about responding to the suffering of Palestinians with courage and tenderness?
3. How can Christians speak honestly about injustice without demonizing people or collapsing into partisan tribalism?
4. What practices help form a heart capable of holding Jewish dignity and Palestinian dignity together?
5. Where is Christ inviting you to step toward compassion, lament, peacemaking, or advocacy?

The Centrality of Jesus Christ for Christian Discipleship and Spirituality

1. What does it mean to say that Christ (not ideology, tribe, or tradition) is the true center of faith and discipleship?
2. Where has your vision of Jesus been too small, too narrow, or too shaped by culture?
3. How does Christ's cruciform love reorder your desires, fears, and sense of purpose?
4. How might your life or community change if every practice, decision, and hope were rooted explicitly in Christ's presence and reign?
5. What does returning to the center look like for you today, and what might Christ be asking you to release, reclaim, or reimagine?

Appendix 2: Would You Help?

Writing a book takes immense effort. It's a sustained labor of love over months, even years. Every page carries hours of thought, prayer, revision, and hope. And while the writing may be solitary, the life of a book is communal. That's where you come in. If this book has meant something to you, I'd be deeply grateful if you could help it find its way into more hands and hearts.

There are two simple but powerful ways you can do that.

First, consider leaving a short review on Amazon (and Goodreads would be wonderful too). Even just a few sentences can help others discover the book, as reviews significantly influence how books are recommended and shared online. You can do that by visiting Amazon or searching for this book and writing a review. Even a short note helps people find the book.

Second, if the book has stirred something in you, would you share it with others: friends, groups, churches, or anyone who might benefit from its message?

Your support helps keep this work going, and it means more than I can say. Thank you for being part of this journey.

Find this book on these pages:
1. Amazon:
https://www.amazon.com.au/stores/author/B008NI4ORQ
2. Goodreads:
https://www.goodreads.com/author/show/20347171.Graham_Joseph
_Hill
3. Author Website:

https://grahamjosephhill.com/books/

Appendix 3: About Me

Graham Joseph Hill (OAM, PhD) is an Adjunct Research Fellow and Associate Professor at Charles Sturt University, and one of Australia's most prolific and awarded Christian authors. He's written more than twenty books, including *Salt, Light, and a City*, which was named Jesus Creed's 2012 Book of the Year (church category); *Healing Our Broken Humanity* (with Grace Ji-Sun Kim), named Outreach Magazine's 2019 Resource of the Year (culture category); and *World Christianity*, shortlisted for the 2025 Australian Christian Book of the Year. In 2024, Graham was awarded the Medal of the Order of Australia (OAM) for his service to theological education. He lives in Sydney with his wife, Shyn.

Author and Ministry Websites

GrahamJosephHill.com
GrahamJosephHill.Substack.com
youtube.com/@GrahamJosephHill_Author
Linktr.ee/dailydevotions
facebook.com/grahamjosephhill/
instagram.com/grahamjosephhill/
amazon.com.au/stores/author/B008NI4ORQ
goodreads.com/author/show/20347171.Graham_Joseph_Hill

Books

See all my books at GrahamJosephHill.com/books

Appendix 4: Connect With Me

I'd love to stay connected with you. You can sign up to my Substack, Spirituality and Society with Hilly, where I share new writing, spiritual reflections, and updates on future books. Please find me on Substack: https://grahamjosephhill.substack.com

You can also find my books on my website:
https://grahamjosephhill.com/books

You can also connect with me through my Facebook author page:
https://www.facebook.com/GrahamJosephHill/